CRACKLE
and Pop!

Dutch text 2018 by Hanna Holwerda
English translation 2021 by Petra van Rijssen

Published by
Lion Hudson Limited
Wilkinson House, Jordan Hill Business Park
Banbury Road, Oxford OX2 8DR, England
www.lionhudson.com

ISBN 978 0 7459 7847 5

First English language edition 2021

Originally published in Dutch under the title "Knetteren en Knallen" by Hanna Holwerda. Copyright © 2018 Uitgeverij Columbus, Heerenveen, The Netherlands. Uitgeverij Columbus is part of Royal Jongbloed Publishers

Acknowledgments
Cover images: Children © YAKOBCHUK VIACHESLAV/shutterstock.com, lab glassware © Vivilweb/Dreamstime.com

Scripture quotations taken from the Holy Bible, New International Version Anglicised. Copyright ©1979, 1984, 2011 Biblica, formerly International Bible Society. Used by permission of Hodder & Stoughton Ltd, an Hachette UK company. All rights reserved. "NIV" is a registered trademark of Biblica. UK trademark number 1448790.

p. 31, Extract taken from the song "Be still for the presence of the Lord" by David J. Evans. Copyright © 1986 Thankyou Music (Adm. by CapitolCMGPublishing.com excl. UK & Europe, adm. by Integrity Music, part of the David C Cook family, songs@integritymusic.com. Reproduced by permission.

A catalogue record for this book is available from the British Library

Printed and bound in China, September 2020, LH54

CRACKLE and Pop!

Bible Science Experiments

HANNA HOLWERDA
TRANSLATED BY PETRA VAN RIJSSEN

INTRODUCTION

A bubbling experiment, a very messy kitchen, and a Bible story! Do these three go together? You might not think so. The Bible is usually read quietly, with everyone sitting around the table, or at bedtime, or in church, isn't it? If you read this book however, you will discover that reading the Bible and doing experiments go together really well. You will understand some of the Bible stories much better and you will discover new things about God, yourself, and the beautiful world in which we live. Have a go and find out for yourself!

For from him and through him and for him are all things.
To him be the glory forever!
Romans 11:36

This book is filled to the brim with experiments that crackle and pop, fizzle and foam. You can try them at home but also on holiday, at a birthday party, on Sunday mornings during children's groups, and, of course, at school! And perhaps these experiments are a great introduction to a Sunday sermon; will anyone volunteer and do a demo during the church service?

Wherever and whenever you roll up your sleeves and try out these experiments, I hope you will be as astonished as I was when I tried them out and discovered what a wonderful God we have.

Hanna Holwerda

TIPS

PEN AND PAPER

Have a pen and a piece of paper at the ready to make notes when you do the experiments, just like a real scientist.

PATIENCE

Sometimes you need to be patient. Not every chemical reaction will fizz, bang, or pop straight away, sometimes it takes a bit more time before something happens.

DO IT AGAIN

For some of the experiments you need to be very precise. Just like in a real lab it is possible that the experiment may not work the first time. In which case, try again!

TOGETHER

Some of the experiments need adult supervision. Please do these ones together. It is not only safer and easier to have an adult there, but it is also a great way to experience and discover something new together. Look out for this red triangle sign.

A BIBLE

There are suggestions of further stories and passages from the Bible to read. Some stories may be more accessible in a Bible for children such as *The Lion First Bible* or *The Lion Bible for Children*.

RISK ASSESSMENT

If using experiments from this book with a group of children, such as in school or in a church group, conduct a risk assessment first. Decide carefully where to do the experiments and plan where to dispose of the chemicals afterwards. For a few of the experiments, it may be sensible for those taking part to wear safety glasses.

INGREDIENTS AND EQUIPMENT

Many of the ingredients and equipment used in the experiments can be found at home. However, some may need to be bought and are available online or in shops, such as supermarkets and pharmacies.

CONTENTS

CONTENTS

AND THERE WAS LIFE

Creation GENESIS 1

MINI ECOSYSTEM

You need: preserving jar, pistachio nut shells, small pebbles, small pieces of charcoal, water in a squeezy bottle, scissors, plant in a pot (small enough to fit in the preserving jar)

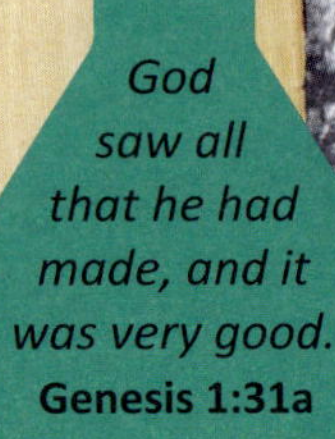

God saw all that he had made, and it was very good.
Genesis 1:31a

Place the small pebbles on the bottom of the preserving jar and add a layer of charcoal. Scatter the pistachio nut shells on top. Remove the plant from its pot and carefully place it on top of the layer of nut shells. Be careful: make sure that the layers don't mix. Add some of the soil from the original plant pot and carefully press it together around the plant. Spray the plant with water, enough to cover the leaves with a thin layer. Pour some water on the soil so it's moist (not too much). Close the lid of the preserving jar so your "mini ecosystem" is air tight. Place the jar in a light and warm spot, but avoid direct sunlight.

What's happening?

A plant absorbs water from the soil with its roots. The tiny, invisible holes in the leaves (pores) release this water again as vapour. The vapour particles cling together and form small droplets, which cling onto the inner wall of the glass jar. Eventually, the drops become too heavy and flow down into the soil, where the roots absorb the water again.

SEED BOMB

You need: packet of flower seed, compost, air-drying modelling clay (e.g. DAS or similar brand), water, dish, scales

Mix about 70g (2.5oz) of seeds with 200g (7oz) of compost.
Add 350g (12oz) of clay and 240ml (8.5fl oz) of water.
Knead and mix everything well together and roll little balls the size of marbles.
Leave your balls to dry in the sun for a day.
Your seed bombs are ready.
Ask yourself: which patches of soil in your neighbourhood could be cheered up with some colourful flowers?
Throw your seed bombs onto the soil, ideally just before it's going to rain.

THE BEST ECOSYSTEM FOR LIFE

Planet Earth offers everything needed for life and survival. Earth is not too close to the sun, so it's not too hot. Nor is it too far from the sun, so it's not too cold. There is water to drink and oxygen to breathe, which are both vital for people, animals, and plants. Earth has an atmosphere, a type of shield that protects it against the sun's harmful rays and burns meteorites, comets, and other space debris.

BREATH OF LIFE

The creation of people GENESIS 2

Then the Lord God formed a man from the dust of the ground and breathed into his nostrils the breath of life, and the man became a living being.
Genesis 2:7

MAKE A BREATHING MACHINE

You need: plastic bottle, 2 red balloons and 1 blue balloon (or different colours), 3 straws, sticky tape, scissors

Cut the bottom out of a bottle. Make two 2cm (⅔in) long cuts in the top of one straw so it splits into two equal halves. Make four cuts in the other side of the straw and fold back all four bits of straw. Cut the other two straws so they each end up 10cm (4in) long. Cut off the thick end of each red balloon (the bit you normally put in your mouth when you blow it up). Slide two 2cm (⅔in) of the 10cm (4in) long straw into each red balloon. Wrap sticky tape around it until it's air tight. Push each of the two straws (now attached to the red balloons) across one half (split) straw. Attach with sticky tape so no air can escape. Make a hole in the bottle top, just big enough to push a straw through. Push the end of the first straw through the top with the end with four cuts sticking out from the top. Fold the four parts around the top and stick them on. Screw the top onto the bottle. The two red balloons are inside the bottle. Attach the top with sticky tape. Blow up the third balloon and let out the air again, so that the balloon is stretched. Cut the balloon in two just over halfway. Make a knot in the balloon (in the usual place). Stretch the other side across the bottom end of the bottle and secure with sticky tape. Your model is finished. Pull down the bottom of the lower balloon to breathe in and push it back up to breathe out. The red balloons will first of all fill with air and will then release the air again, just like your lungs when you breathe.

What's happening?

This experiment demonstrates what happens inside your body when you breathe. The bottle is like your chest, with lungs on each side (the red balloons). When you breathe in, your lungs expand and your midriff (the front of the body between the chest and the waist) contracts and then moves down. Just like when you pull the balloon at the bottom. When you breathe out, your midriff moves up again and your lungs shrink.

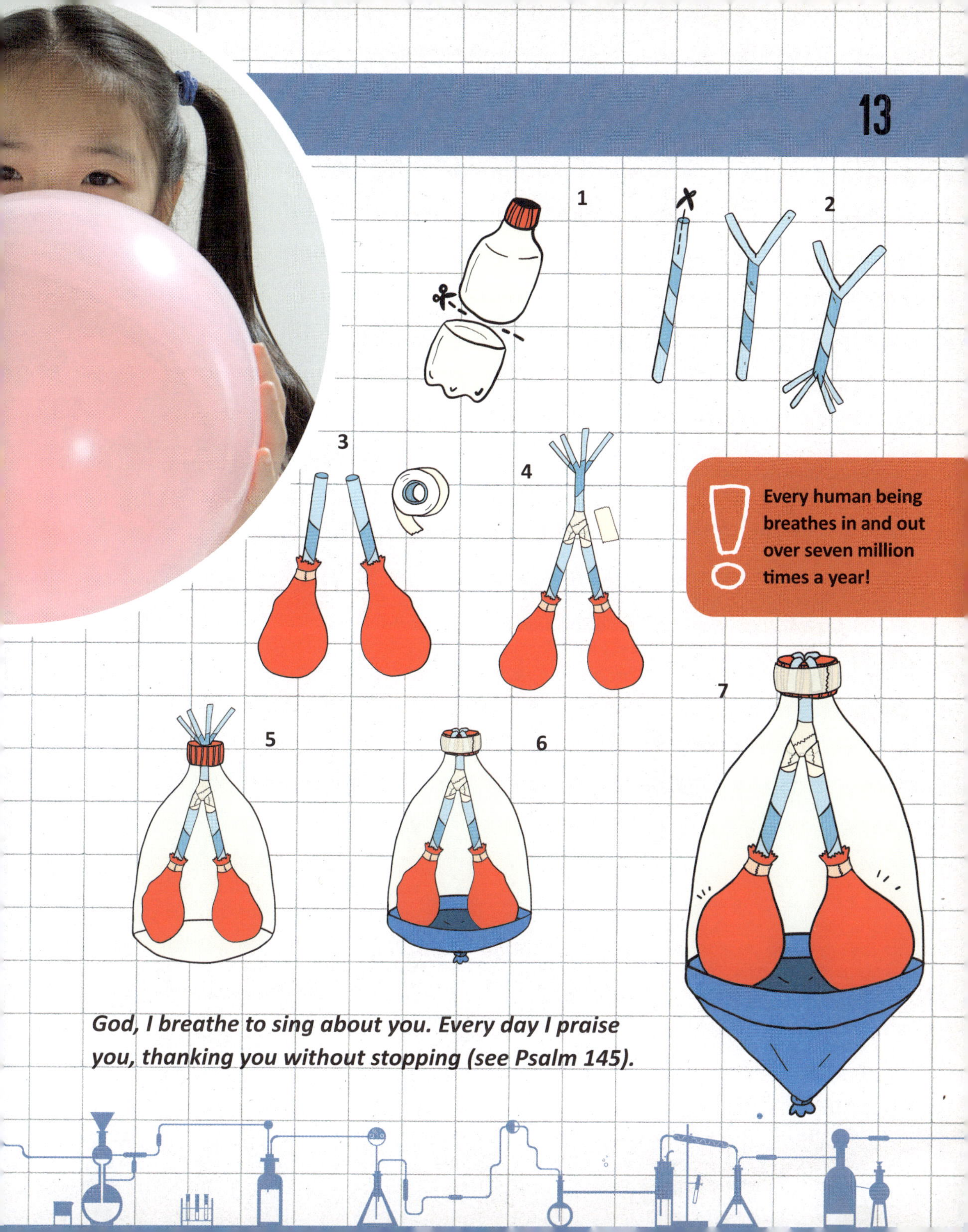

Every human being breathes in and out over seven million times a year!

God, I breathe to sing about you. Every day I praise you, thanking you without stopping (see Psalm 145).

YOUR OWN BUILDING BLOCKS

A song all about us PSALM 139

Read all of Psalm 139 together.

For you created my inmost being; you knit me together in my mother's womb. I praise you because I am fearfully and wonderfully made; your works are wonderful, I know that full well.
Psalm 139:13–14

DISCOVER YOUR OWN DNA

You need: glass filled with 240ml (8.5fl oz) of water, salt, teaspoon, empty glass, liquid soap, disinfectant (with alcohol, available from the pharmacy), magnifying glass

Add one teaspoon of salt to the glass of water and stir. Put a spoonful of salt in your mouth. Don't swallow, just rinse with water and bite the inside of your cheeks. Spit the water into the empty glass. Add one teaspoon of liquid soap and stir very carefully. Add 2–3 teaspoons of disinfectant. It should form a layer on top of the soap and spit solution. Make sure you don't stir and don't even touch the mixture with your spoon!

Wait for a few minutes. Can you see a type of slime in between the two liquids? This is your DNA. Have a look at it with a magnifying glass.

What's happening?

By rinsing your mouth with salty water, the DNA in your gums dislodges and ends up in the liquid. When you spit it out, the DNA ends up in the glass. The liquid soap breaks down the cell wall and that of the nucleus inside the cell and now the DNA can escape. The alcohol in the disinfectant helps the DNA to separate from the rest of the cell. You can see DNA when it's loose like this.

WHAT IS DNA?

Your body is made up of lots and lots of tiny cells. In each cell there is a nucleus which contains your DNA. This DNA looks like a twisted ladder. The ladder contains a code and each human being has a different code. We are all unique.

God made people unique. You are unique!

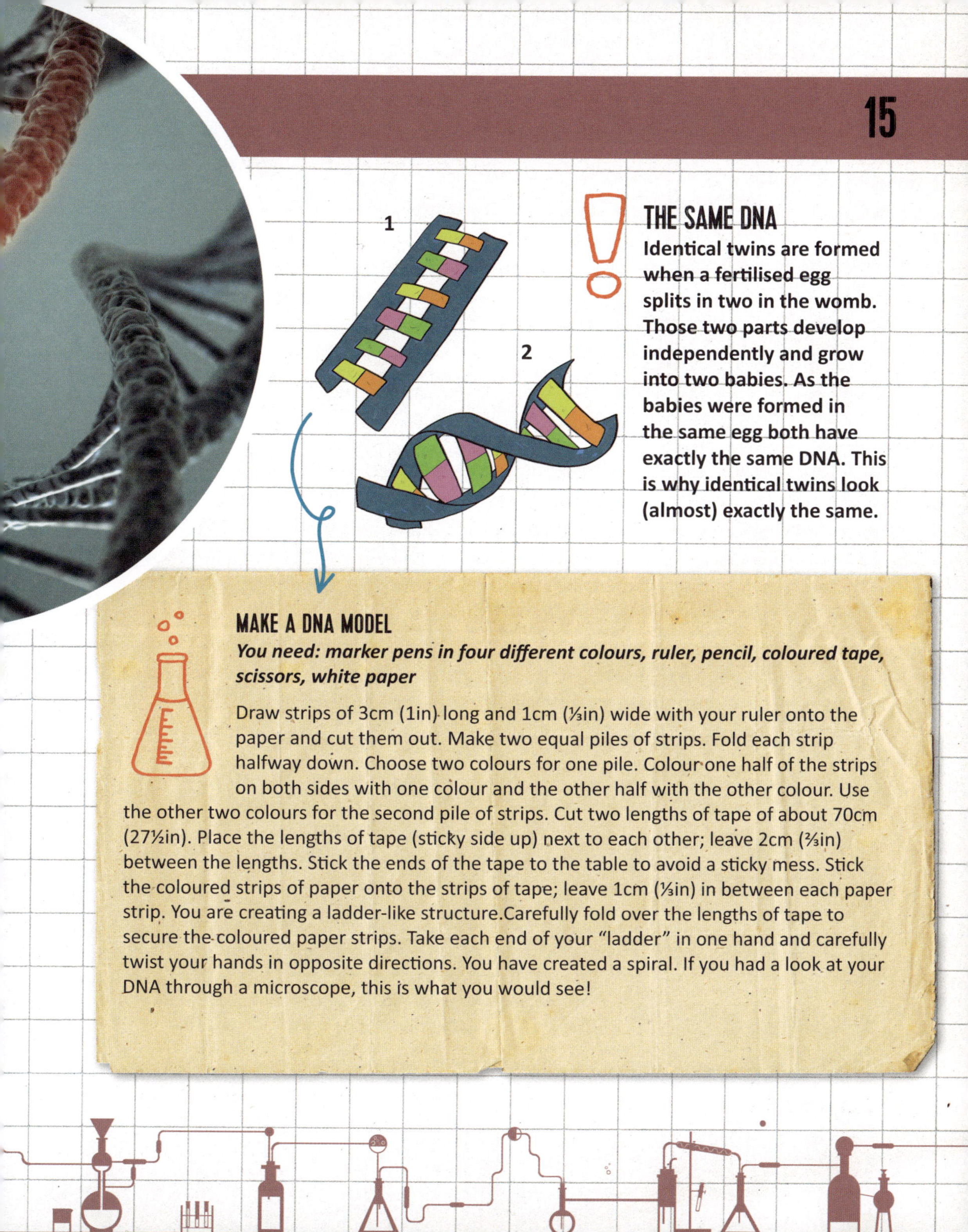

THE SAME DNA

Identical twins are formed when a fertilised egg splits in two in the womb. Those two parts develop independently and grow into two babies. As the babies were formed in the same egg both have exactly the same DNA. This is why identical twins look (almost) exactly the same.

MAKE A DNA MODEL

You need: marker pens in four different colours, ruler, pencil, coloured tape, scissors, white paper

Draw strips of 3cm (1in) long and 1cm (⅓in) wide with your ruler onto the paper and cut them out. Make two equal piles of strips. Fold each strip halfway down. Choose two colours for one pile. Colour one half of the strips on both sides with one colour and the other half with the other colour. Use the other two colours for the second pile of strips. Cut two lengths of tape of about 70cm (27½in). Place the lengths of tape (sticky side up) next to each other; leave 2cm (⅔in) between the lengths. Stick the ends of the tape to the table to avoid a sticky mess. Stick the coloured strips of paper onto the strips of tape; leave 1cm (⅓in) in between each paper strip. You are creating a ladder-like structure.Carefully fold over the lengths of tape to secure the coloured paper strips. Take each end of your "ladder" in one hand and carefully twist your hands in opposite directions. You have created a spiral. If you had a look at your DNA through a microscope, this is what you would see!

ENDLESS RAIN

Noah's ark GENESIS 7 AND 8

Read the story of Noah's ark.

The Lord then said to Noah, "Go into the ark, you and your whole family, because I have found you righteous in this generation.... Seven days from now I will send rain on the earth for forty days and forty nights, and I will wipe from the face of the earth every living creature I have made."
Genesis 7:1 and 4

CAN A BOAT FLOAT?

You need: glass jar or dish with water, some soft clay, and some marbles

Fill the glass jar with water. Split the clay and roll it into two small balls. Place one ball onto the water. Does it float? Place a marble onto the water. What happens next? Remove both the clay ball and marble from the water. Flatten the other (dry) ball of clay and shape it into a small, shallow cup. Place this onto the water. What is happening now? Place the marble onto the clay cup. Does it still float?

Question: how many marbles can the clay "boat" hold without sinking?

What's happening?

The floating of the small objects is possible because of the water's "surface tension". The water pushes against the clay. As it's relatively heavy, the clay pushes back. The ball of clay only has a small area that touches the water, so the effect of the pushing water is small. The clay is stronger and heavier than water. The clay ball sinks. If you increase the contact area between the clay and the water, for instance by making a cup shape, the water is more powerful as it pushes against a larger surface. The clay boat floats, even if you add marbles.

FLOATING OR SINKING

You need: plant based oil, water, large glass or glass jar, small toy brick, coin, and other small objects

Half fill the glass with water.
Carefully add oil until 3cm (1in) below the edge of the glass. The two layers of liquid must not mix. Add the small objects one by one. Are they floating?

What's happening?

Oil and water don't mix as they push each other away. Oil is lighter than water and so it floats on water. Oil and water have different surface tensions. Water is stronger and pushes harder against objects, so some things float on water but sink in oil.

MAKE A BOAT

You can create little boats using different materials and test which ones float best and for the longest time. You can use cork, paper, scrubbing brushes, ice lolly sticks etc.

A COLOURFUL RAINBOW

Noah's ark GENESIS 7 AND 8

Then God said to Noah, "Come out of the ark, you and your wife and your sons and their wives. Bring out every kind of living creature that is with you – the birds, the animals, and all the creatures that move along the ground – so they can multiply on the earth and be fruitful and increase in number on it."
Genesis 8:15–17

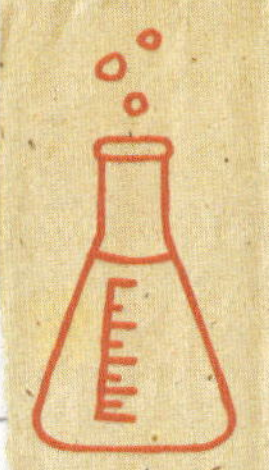

CREATE A RAINBOW

You need: simple round wine glass (with a stem and a foot), water, desk lamp, white paper

Fill the glass with water and place it on the edge of the paper. Focus the lamp onto the glass from an angle, so the light shines through the glass and onto the paper. Can you see a rainbow?

Tip: Sometimes the rainbow isn't immediately visible. If it isn't, carefully move the white paper or the lamp and try again.

Is it sunny outside? Create a rainbow in your garden.

You need: hose or plant spray (mister), water, sunshine

Go outside. Turn your back towards the sun. Make sure only very little drops of water (like mist) come out of the hose or spray. You should be able to adjust this. Spray water up into the sky. Small droplets of water show a rainbow.

What is happening?

A ray of light looks white but it isn't. Light is made up of all the colours of the rainbow. These colours mixed together appear white. But when the light shines through water, the ray of light is "broken" and "pulled apart". This way, each individual colour is made visible. You will see a rainbow. Outside a rainbow forms in the same way when the sun shines onto small water droplets.

Whenever I bring clouds over the earth and the rainbow appears in the clouds, I will remember my covenant between me and you and all living creatures of every kind. Never again will the waters become a flood to destroy all life.
Genesis 9:14–15

ASK AN ADULT TO HELP YOU.

CREATE A RAIN GAUGE

You need: large plastic bottle, sharp knife, permanent marker, ruler, notebook, pen

Ask an adult to cut the top third off the bottle. Place the cut off top upside down onto the bottom bit of the cut bottle (like a funnel). Lean the ruler against the bottle and mark centimetres (or inches) onto the bottle with the permanent pen.

Place your rain gauge in the garden in a fixed spot and each day write down in your notebook how much rain has fallen. Remember to empty it once you have taken the reading.

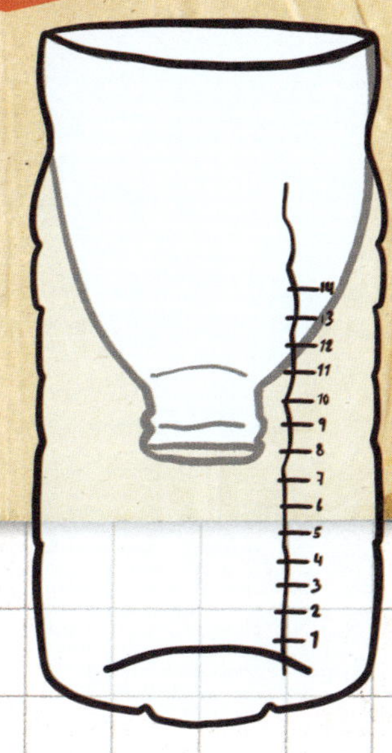

THE SPEED OF LIGHT

Light travels at a speed of 299,792km (186,282 miles) per second. If you were able to run as fast as light, you could run around the earth seven times in about one second.

WHY ARE RAIN CLOUDS GREY?

Clouds are made out of many, many raindrops. The more raindrops there are in a cloud, the more grey the cloud will seem. This is because the sun's light rays are not, or hardly, able to shine through the cloud. So the greyer the cloud, the bigger the chance of rain!

GOD'S PLAN FOR ABRAM

Abram, father of a large nation GENESIS 15

God has a plan for Abram, but Abram is impatient! Things aren't going how he had imagined.

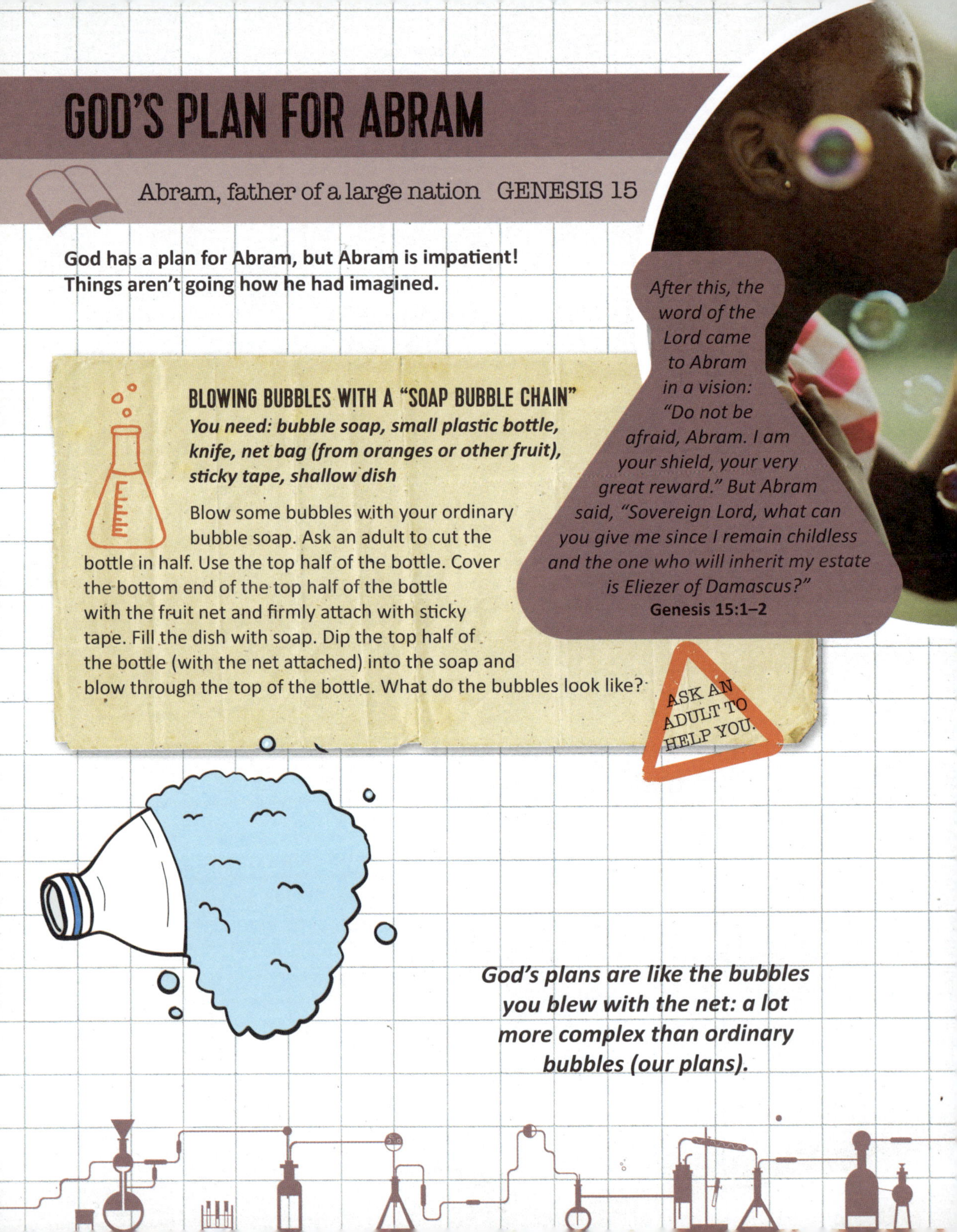

After this, the word of the Lord came to Abram in a vision: "Do not be afraid, Abram. I am your shield, your very great reward." But Abram said, "Sovereign Lord, what can you give me since I remain childless and the one who will inherit my estate is Eliezer of Damascus?"
Genesis 15:1–2

BLOWING BUBBLES WITH A "SOAP BUBBLE CHAIN"

You need: bubble soap, small plastic bottle, knife, net bag (from oranges or other fruit), sticky tape, shallow dish

Blow some bubbles with your ordinary bubble soap. Ask an adult to cut the bottle in half. Use the top half of the bottle. Cover the bottom end of the top half of the bottle with the fruit net and firmly attach with sticky tape. Fill the dish with soap. Dip the top half of the bottle (with the net attached) into the soap and blow through the top of the bottle. What do the bubbles look like?

ASK AN ADULT TO HELP YOU.

God's plans are like the bubbles you blew with the net: a lot more complex than ordinary bubbles (our plans).

A further thought:

God's plans: we only see what appears on the surface, but there is a lot more that we can't see.

Only a tenth of an iceberg's volume is seen above water.

YOU COULD ALSO COMPARE GOD'S PLANS WITH THE ICE CUBE IN THE FOLLOWING EXPERIMENT.

You need: glass of water, ice cube

Put the ice cube into the glass. Look at the ice cube through the side of the glass. How much of the ice cube sticks out above the water and how much is immersed?

UNIQUE FINGERPRINT?

Jacob or Esau GENESIS 27

Jacob and Esau are twins, but they are very different. Jacob, the younger twin is jealous because he thinks that Esau is about to receive the greatest blessing. Together with his mother he comes up with a plan. He dresses up as his brother and tricks his blind father into giving him the blessing destined for the firstborn child.

Read the whole story about Jacob and Esau and their father's blessing in Genesis 25:19–34 and 27:1–35.

Jacob said to Rebekah his mother, "But my brother Esau is a hairy man while I have smooth skin." She also covered his hands and the smooth part of his neck with the goatskins. Then Isaac said to Jacob, "Come near so I can touch you, my son, to know whether you really are my son Esau or not."
Genesis 27:11, 16 and 21

FINGERPRINTS

You need: ink pad, sheet of paper

Your fingerprint is unique. Nobody has the same fingerprint. Police and detectives use fingerprints to track down people. Push your finger gently into the ink and then onto the paper. Compare your fingerprint with someone else's, a friend or family member. How many differences can you spot?

Tip: Take photos of the prints and blow them up. This way you can compare even more carefully!

Can you swap fingerprints so you won't be found out? A bit like Jacob when he tried to look like his brother by wrapping his arms and neck in goat skins?

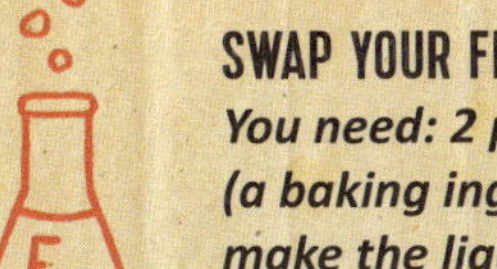

SWAP YOUR FINGERPRINT

You need: 2 people, 2 bits of modelling clay, liquid gelatine (a baking ingredient). Follow the packet instructions to make the liquid.

Roll two small balls of clay. Each person presses their right-hand index finger into their clay ball. Pour a bit of the liquid gelatine onto the clay ball, covering the fingerprint. Leave the balls in the fridge for about 15 minutes.
Remember to label each ball, so you know which one is which.
Remove the clay from the fridge and carefully lift the gelatine off the clay. Look at your fingerprint on the gelatine. Give each other your jelly fingerprints and place these on your index fingers. You have now successfully swapped fingerprints!

Did you know that your tongue has a unique print too? It's just a lot more tricky to produce a tongue print.

YOU WON'T BE TRICKED THAT EASILY...

A fingerprint is not the only thing that gives away someone's identity. Think about the story of Jacob and Esau.

***Scent*: Esau's clothes had absorbed his body odour and the smell of the fields and woods. (see Genesis 27:27)**
***Voice*: Jacob's voice remained the same and this is what made his father doubt so much. (see Genesis 27:22)**

GOD PROTECTS YOU

Jacob's dream in Bethel GENESIS 28

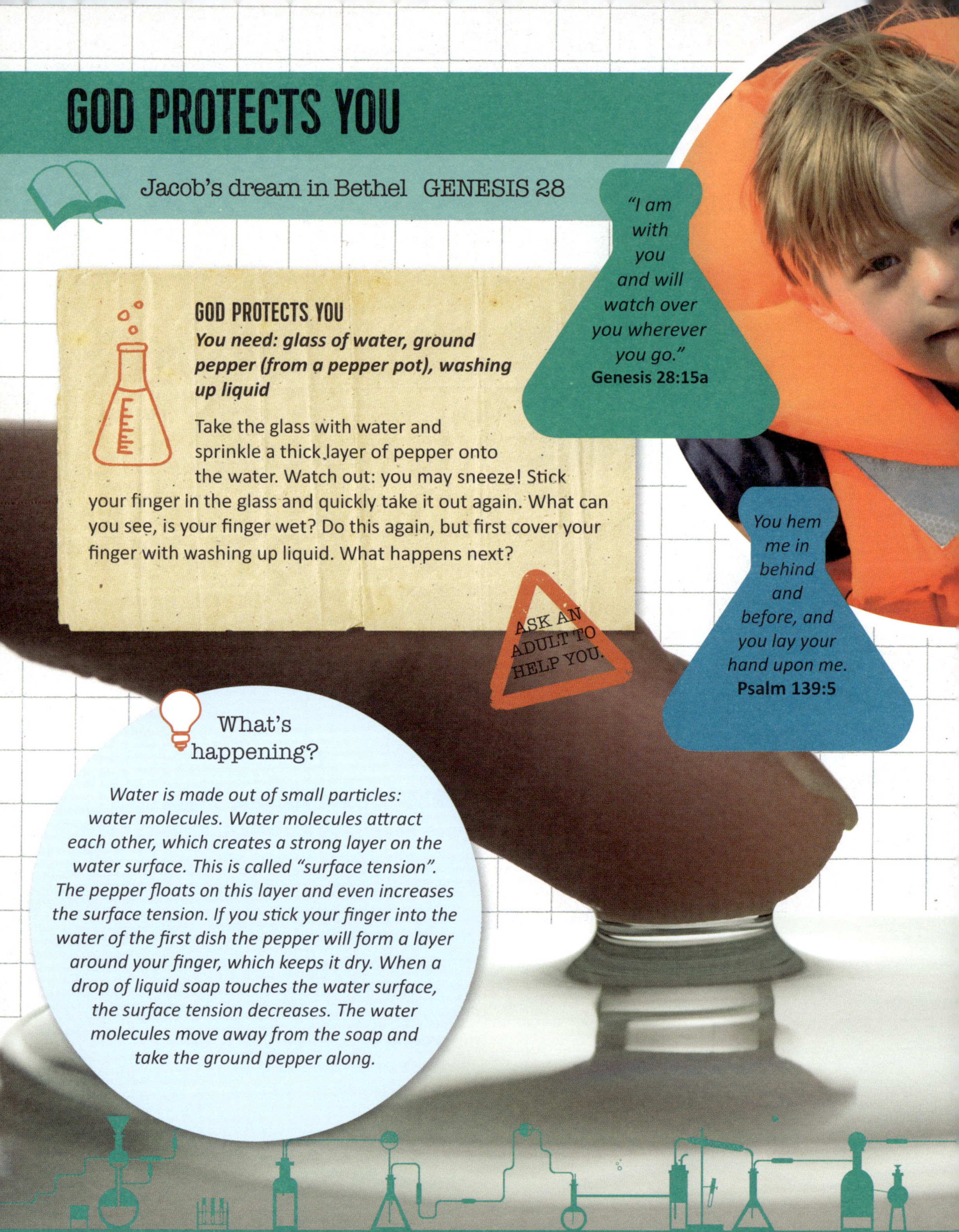

GOD PROTECTS YOU

You need: glass of water, ground pepper (from a pepper pot), washing up liquid

Take the glass with water and sprinkle a thick layer of pepper onto the water. Watch out: you may sneeze! Stick your finger in the glass and quickly take it out again. What can you see, is your finger wet? Do this again, but first cover your finger with washing up liquid. What happens next?

ASK AN ADULT TO HELP YOU.

"I am with you and will watch over you wherever you go."
Genesis 28:15a

You hem me in behind and before, and you lay your hand upon me.
Psalm 139:5

What's happening?

Water is made out of small particles: water molecules. Water molecules attract each other, which creates a strong layer on the water surface. This is called "surface tension". The pepper floats on this layer and even increases the surface tension. If you stick your finger into the water of the first dish the pepper will form a layer around your finger, which keeps it dry. When a drop of liquid soap touches the water surface, the surface tension decreases. The water molecules move away from the soap and take the ground pepper along.

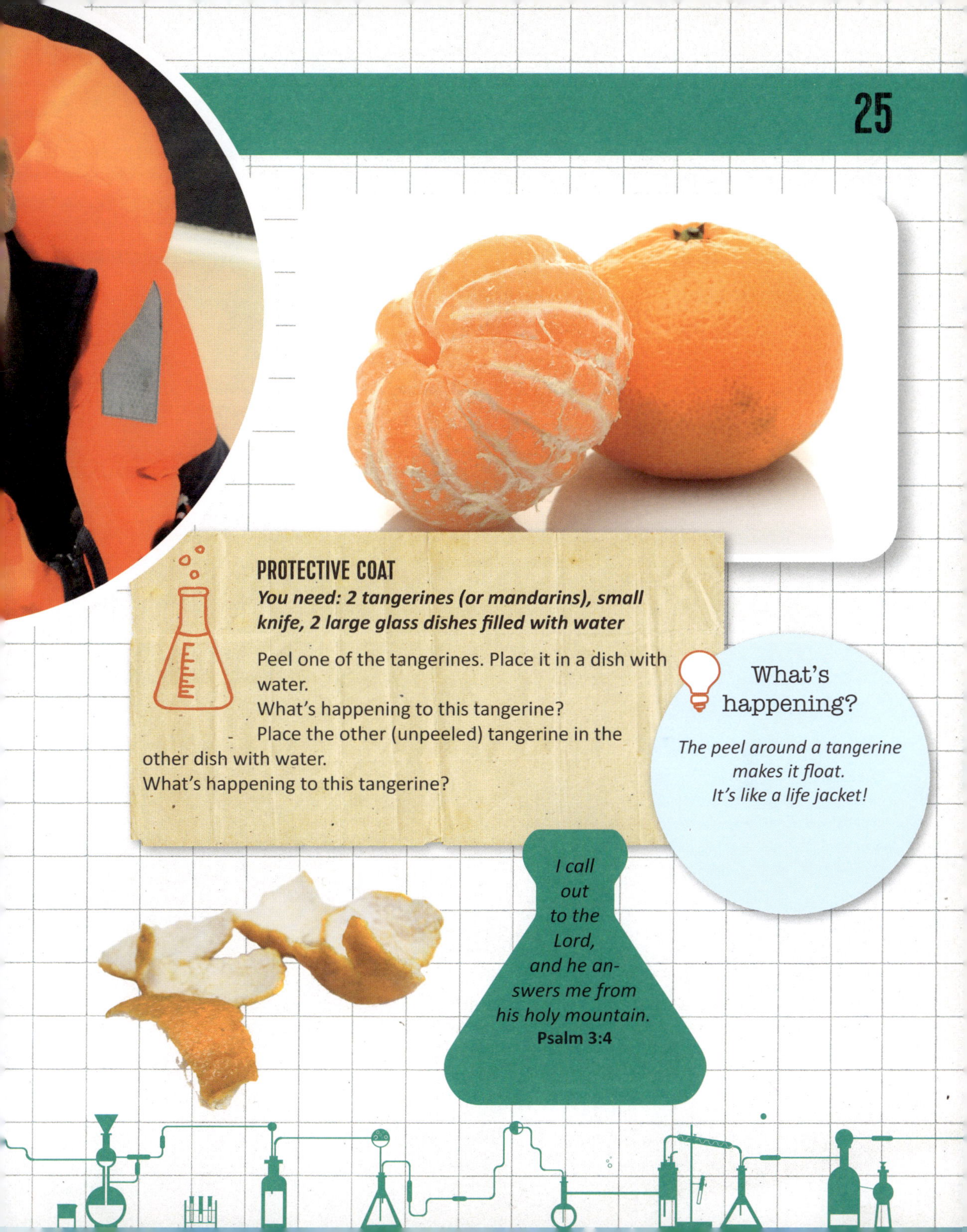

PROTECTIVE COAT

You need: 2 tangerines (or mandarins), small knife, 2 large glass dishes filled with water

Peel one of the tangerines. Place it in a dish with water.

What's happening to this tangerine?

Place the other (unpeeled) tangerine in the other dish with water.

What's happening to this tangerine?

What's happening?

The peel around a tangerine makes it float. It's like a life jacket!

I call out to the Lord, and he answers me from his holy mountain.
Psalm 3:4

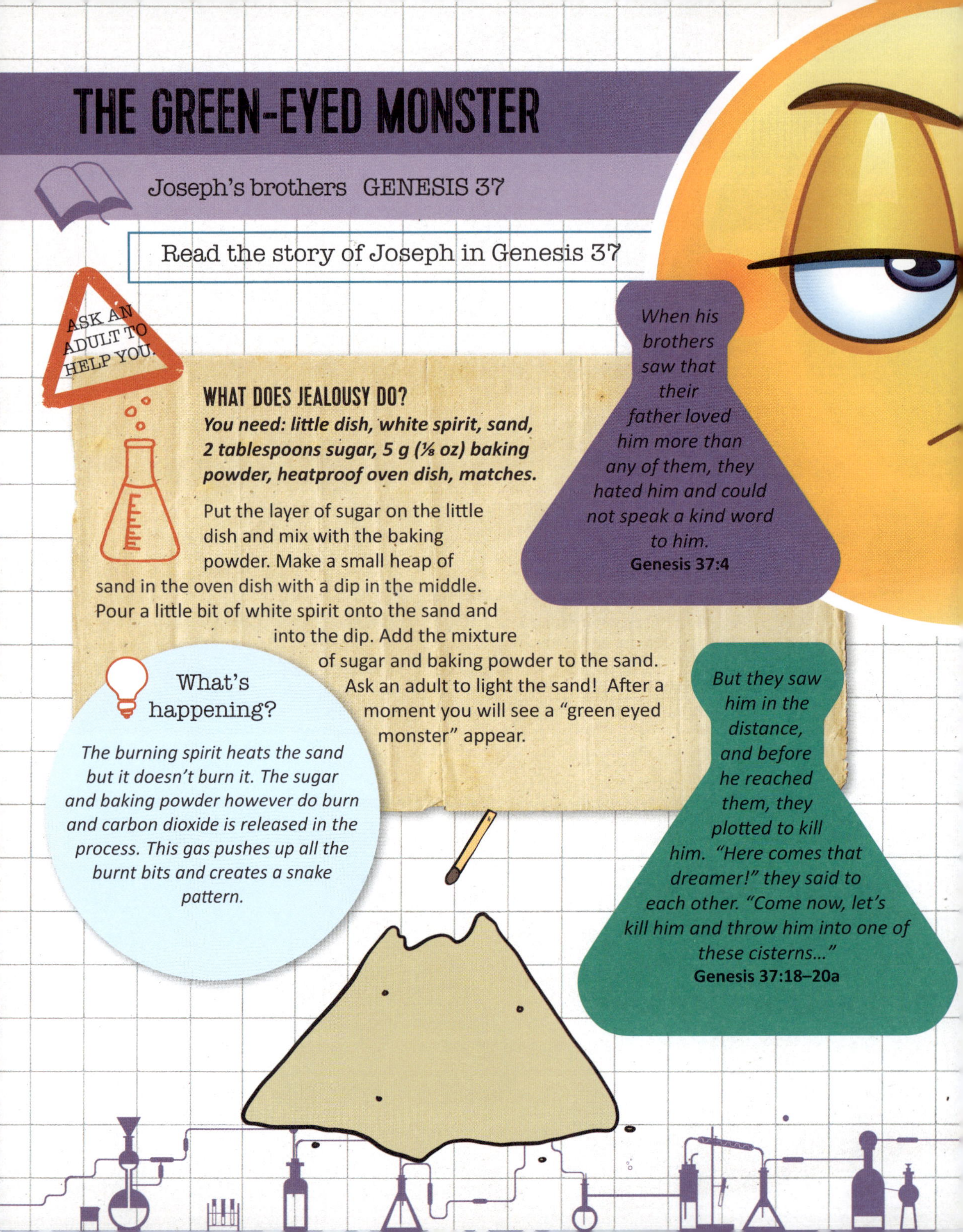

THE GREEN-EYED MONSTER

Joseph's brothers GENESIS 37

Read the story of Joseph in Genesis 37

ASK AN ADULT TO HELP YOU.

WHAT DOES JEALOUSY DO?

You need: little dish, white spirit, sand, 2 tablespoons sugar, 5 g (⅛ oz) baking powder, heatproof oven dish, matches.

Put the layer of sugar on the little dish and mix with the baking powder. Make a small heap of sand in the oven dish with a dip in the middle. Pour a little bit of white spirit onto the sand and into the dip. Add the mixture of sugar and baking powder to the sand. Ask an adult to light the sand! After a moment you will see a "green eyed monster" appear.

When his brothers saw that their father loved him more than any of them, they hated him and could not speak a kind word to him.
Genesis 37:4

What's happening?

The burning spirit heats the sand but it doesn't burn it. The sugar and baking powder however do burn and carbon dioxide is released in the process. This gas pushes up all the burnt bits and creates a snake pattern.

But they saw him in the distance, and before he reached them, they plotted to kill him. "Here comes that dreamer!" they said to each other. "Come now, let's kill him and throw him into one of these cisterns..."
Genesis 37:18–20a

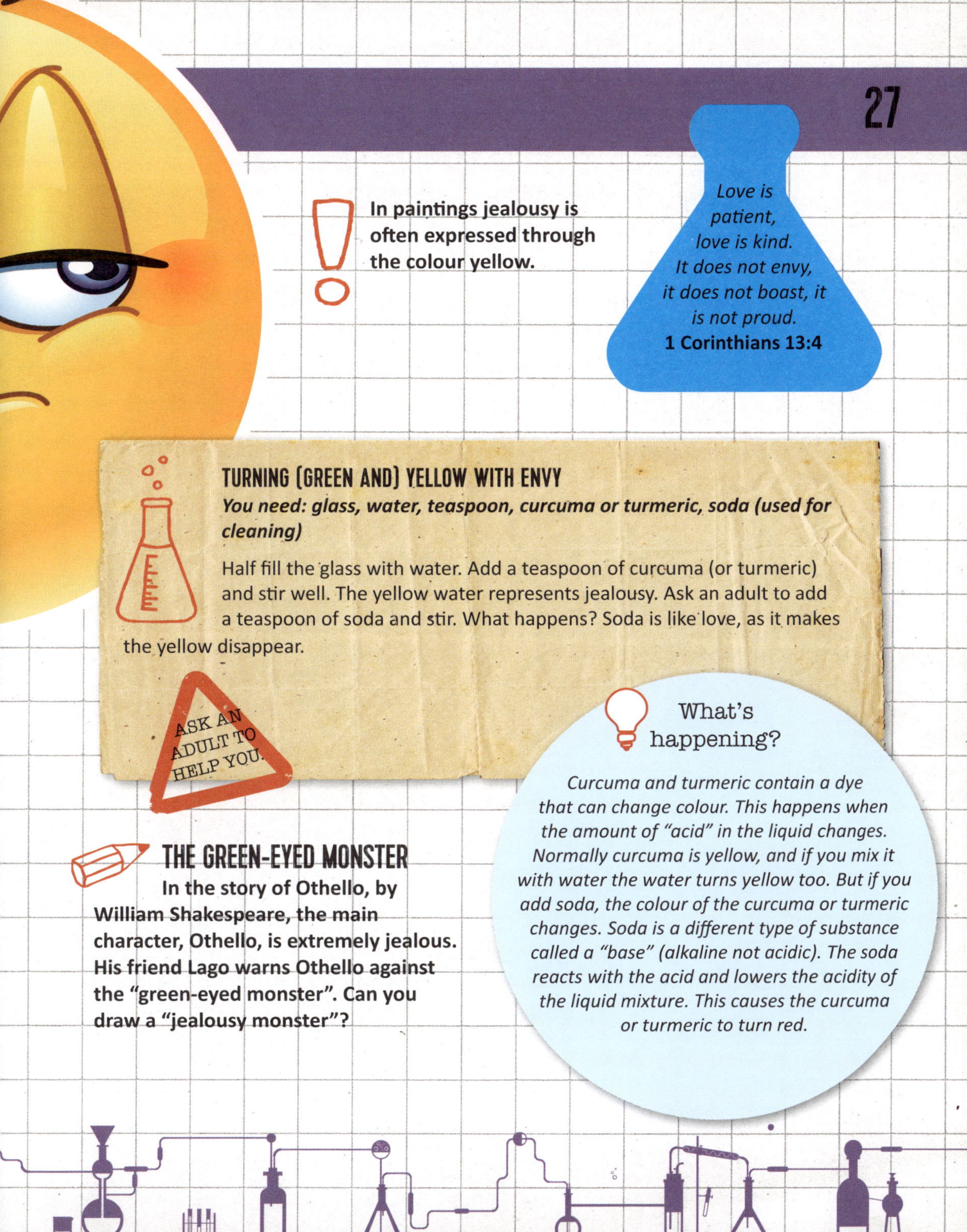

In paintings jealousy is often expressed through the colour yellow.

Love is patient, love is kind. It does not envy, it does not boast, it is not proud.
1 Corinthians 13:4

TURNING (GREEN AND) YELLOW WITH ENVY

You need: glass, water, teaspoon, curcuma or turmeric, soda (used for cleaning)

Half fill the glass with water. Add a teaspoon of curcuma (or turmeric) and stir well. The yellow water represents jealousy. Ask an adult to add a teaspoon of soda and stir. What happens? Soda is like love, as it makes the yellow disappear.

ASK AN ADULT TO HELP YOU.

What's happening?

Curcuma and turmeric contain a dye that can change colour. This happens when the amount of "acid" in the liquid changes. Normally curcuma is yellow, and if you mix it with water the water turns yellow too. But if you add soda, the colour of the curcuma or turmeric changes. Soda is a different type of substance called a "base" (alkaline not acidic). The soda reacts with the acid and lowers the acidity of the liquid mixture. This causes the curcuma or turmeric to turn red.

THE GREEN-EYED MONSTER

In the story of Othello, by William Shakespeare, the main character, Othello, is extremely jealous. His friend Lago warns Othello against the "green-eyed monster". Can you draw a "jealousy monster"?

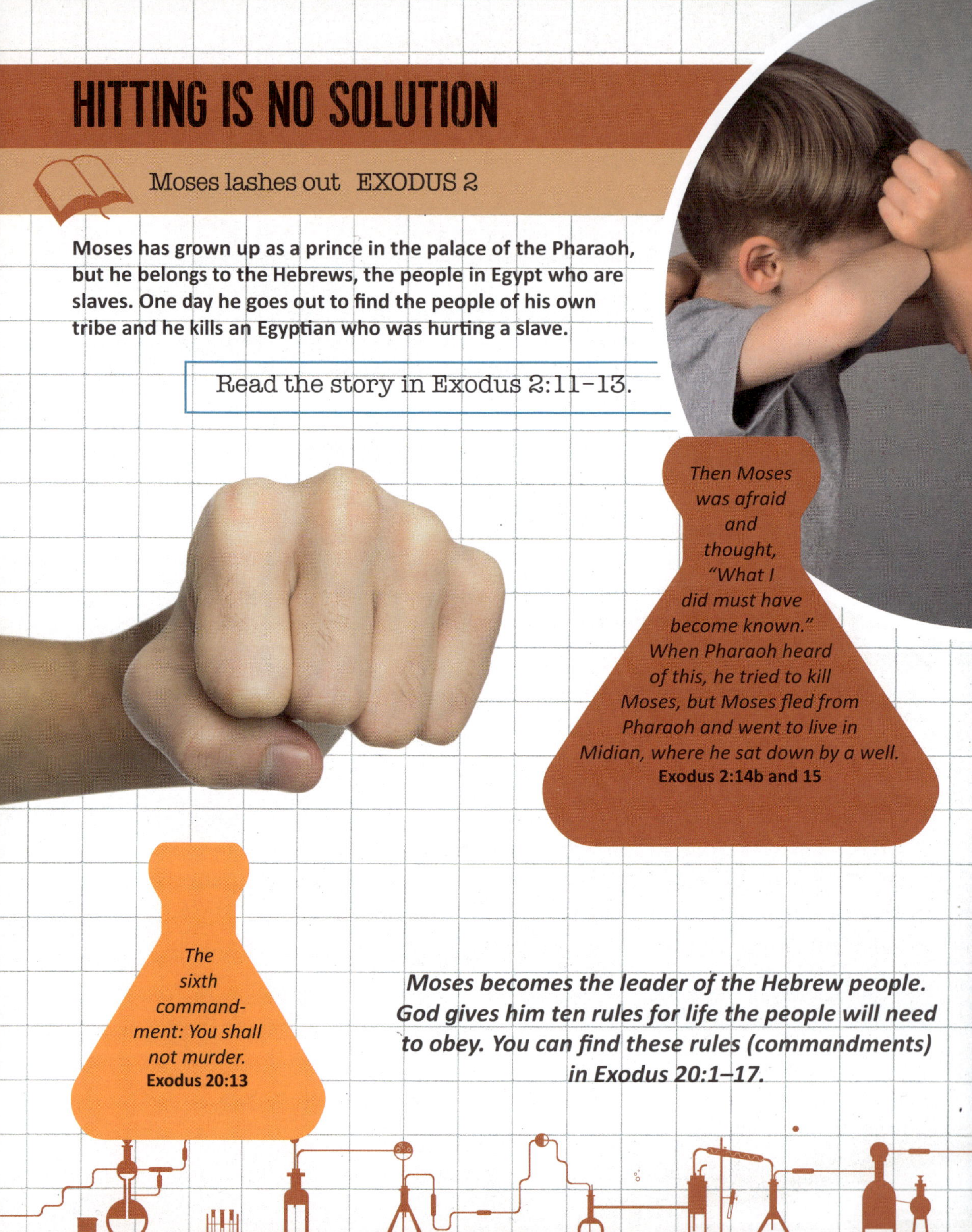

HITTING IS NO SOLUTION

Moses lashes out EXODUS 2

Moses has grown up as a prince in the palace of the Pharaoh, but he belongs to the Hebrews, the people in Egypt who are slaves. One day he goes out to find the people of his own tribe and he kills an Egyptian who was hurting a slave.

Read the story in Exodus 2:11–13.

Then Moses was afraid and thought, "What I did must have become known." When Pharaoh heard of this, he tried to kill Moses, but Moses fled from Pharaoh and went to live in Midian, where he sat down by a well.
Exodus 2:14b and 15

The sixth commandment: You shall not murder.
Exodus 20:13

Moses becomes the leader of the Hebrew people. God gives him ten rules for life the people will need to obey. You can find these rules (commandments) in Exodus 20:1–17.

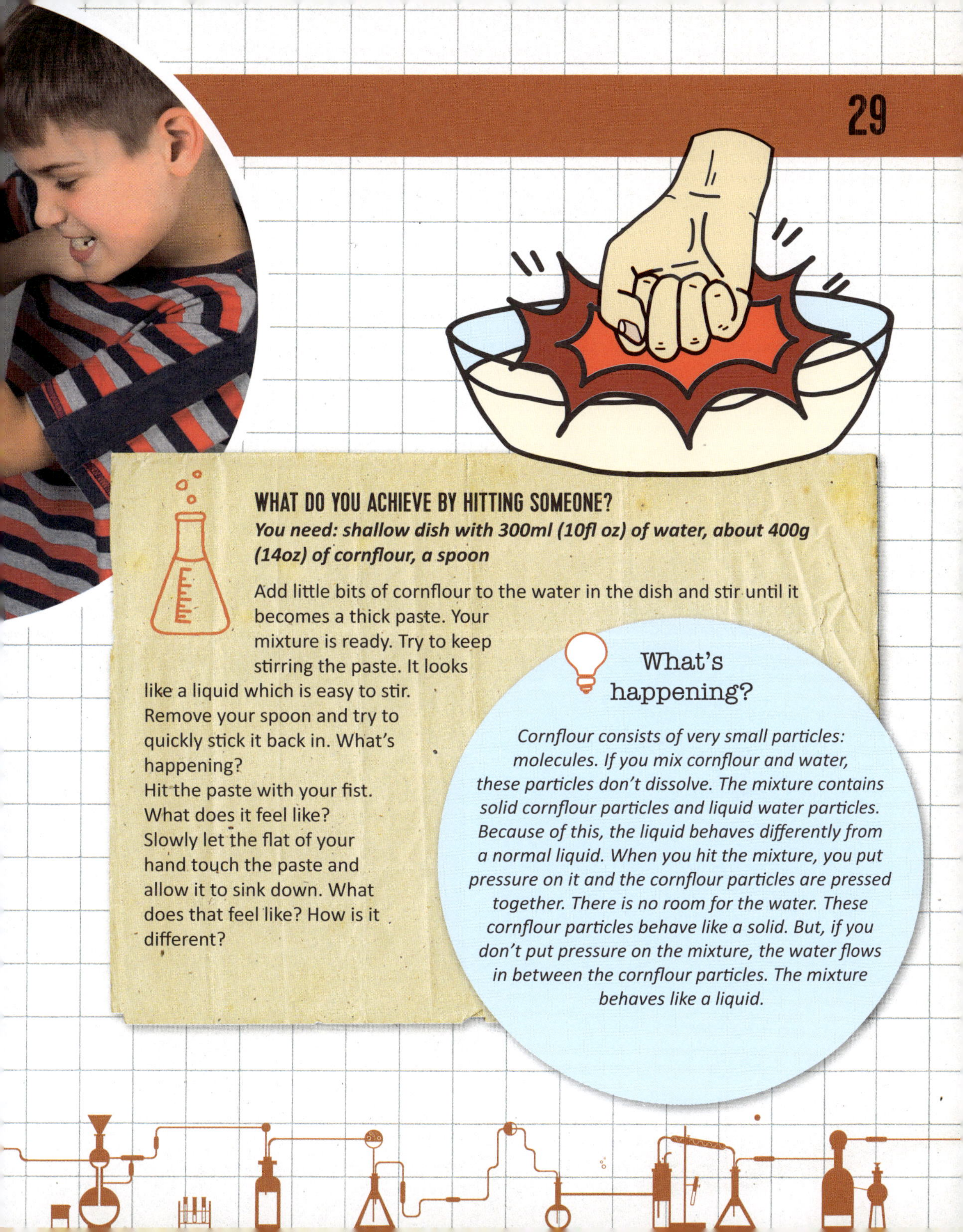

WHAT DO YOU ACHIEVE BY HITTING SOMEONE?

You need: shallow dish with 300ml (10fl oz) of water, about 400g (14oz) of cornflour, a spoon

Add little bits of cornflour to the water in the dish and stir until it becomes a thick paste. Your mixture is ready. Try to keep stirring the paste. It looks like a liquid which is easy to stir. Remove your spoon and try to quickly stick it back in. What's happening?

Hit the paste with your fist. What does it feel like? Slowly let the flat of your hand touch the paste and allow it to sink down. What does that feel like? How is it different?

What's happening?

Cornflour consists of very small particles: molecules. If you mix cornflour and water, these particles don't dissolve. The mixture contains solid cornflour particles and liquid water particles. Because of this, the liquid behaves differently from a normal liquid. When you hit the mixture, you put pressure on it and the cornflour particles are pressed together. There is no room for the water. These cornflour particles behave like a solid. But, if you don't put pressure on the mixture, the water flows in between the cornflour particles. The mixture behaves like a liquid.

STRANGE FIRE

Moses and the burning bush EXODUS 3

There the angel of the Lord appeared to him in flames of fire from within a bush. Moses saw that though the bush was on fire it did not burn up.
Exodus 3:2

THE BUSH THAT DOESN'T BURN

You need: green paper, water, white spirit, salt, small dish, spoon, pliers, match or lighter

Half fill the dish with water, add a big spoonful of salt and add white spirit until the dish is full. Stir very well. Cut a bush shape out of the green piece of paper. Immerse the shape into the mixture. Ask an adult to hold the bush with the pliers and set it alight.

Tip: If you don't have pliers, you can pierce the bush with a fork.

ASK AN ADULT TO HELP YOU.

What's happening?

The paper bush starts to flame but doesn't burn. The water in the mixture fills the paper and prevents burning. Only the spirit will burn.

Spirit is a Latin word for "breath" and for breathing in and out. Do you think that makes sense?

Be still for the glory of the Lord
Is shining all around
He burns with holy fire
With splendour He is crowned

How awesome is the sight
Our radiant King of Light
Be still for the glory of the Lord
Is shining all around

(From: Be still for the presence of the Lord)

Tip: Sing this song outside and with bare feet.

What do you think "holy ground" means?

When the Lord saw that he had gone over to look, God called to him from within the bush, "Moses! Moses!" And Moses said, "Here I am." "Do not come any closer," God said. "Take off your sandals, for the place where you are standing is holy ground."
Exodus 3:4–5

IN THE LIGHT

The exodus from Egypt EXODUS 14

God protects the people of Israel by "shining his light upon them" and leaving the Egyptians in the dark.

LIGHT AND DARKNESS

You need: 2 small plates, cotton wool, water, cress seed

Place a layer of cotton wool on each plate and add some water. Sprinkle the cress seed onto the cotton wool. Make sure the seed is shared equally between the plates. Place one of the plates in a sunny spot and the other one in a dark spot. Make sure the cotton wool remains moist. Follow what happens over a few days. Can you see any difference between the seeds on the different plates?

What's happening?

A plant needs three things to grow: water, light, and carbon dioxide, a gas it absorbs from the air. Leaves contain a substance named chlorophyll which "catch" the light. Light is an energy source. The plant uses this energy to make sugar out of water and carbon dioxide. This is called "photosynthesis". Without light there is not enough energy for the plant to make sugar and plants need sugar as their food source.

The pillar of cloud also moved from in front and stood behind them, coming between the armies of Egypt and Israel. Throughout the night the cloud brought darkness to the one side and light to the other; so neither went near the other all night long.

Exodus 14:19b–20

Then Moses stretched out his hand over the sea, and all that night the Lord drove the sea back with a strong east wind and turned it into dry land. The waters were divided, and the Israelites went through the sea on dry ground, with a wall of water on their right and on their left.

Exodus 14:21–22

ASK AN ADULT TO HELP YOU!

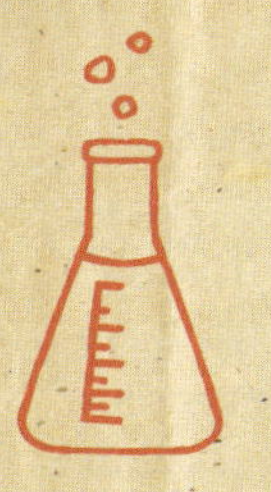

WATER AND WIND

You need: glass oven dish, hair dryer, water, brown paper

Put some water in the oven dish (a shallow layer) and place the dish on the brown paper. Turn on the hairdryer (most powerful setting) and blow against the water.

Tip: Add a few drops of blue food colouring or ecoline (liquid watercolour paint) to the water and mix.

MAP OF MOSES' LIFE (DEUTERONOMY 32)

Mediterranean Sea
Mount Nebo
Moab
GOSHEN
desert
Nile
Red Sea
Mount Sinai
EGYPT
Midian

"Do not fear, for I have redeemed you; I have summoned you by name; you are mine. When you pass through the waters, I will be with you; and when you pass through the rivers, they will not sweep over you."
Isaiah 43:1b and 2a

Do you know where the Sea of Reeds (part of the Red Sea), which the people of Israel crossed, is?

The Sea of Reeds was probably the northern part of the Red Sea. The Red Sea used to stretch further north than where the Gulf of Suez reaches. It probably stretched as far as the Great Bitter Lake, a long and thin saltwater lake in Egypt.

TOXIC WORDS

Balaam tries to curse the people of Israel
NUMBERS 22 AND 23

Sometimes people say that words don't hurt. But is this true? Words can hurt our feelings a lot. What happens when a friend says poisonous words to you? You can compare the effects with what happens in the next experiment.

Read the story of Balaam. King Balak is afraid of the people of Israel. He asks Balaam to curse the people of Israel so he can defeat them. Will Balaam succeed when speaking poisonous words over the people?

You can find this story in Numbers 22:5–6 and 23:7–12.

Do not let any unwholesome talk come out of your mouths, but only what is helpful for building others up according to their needs, that it may benefit those who listen.
Ephesians 4:29

ROTTEN INSIDE

You need: 2 apples, spoon, small sharp knife

Throw one apple on the floor (just once) and hit it with the back of a spoon. Hit it with your fist. Put the beaten apple next to the untouched one and compare the two. What differences can you see?
Cut open both apples. What do you see?
Perhaps you can't tell from the outside that one apple has been dropped and hit, but inside something has happened. This is what arguments, bullying and poisonous words can do to people.

ASK AN ADULT TO HELP YOU.

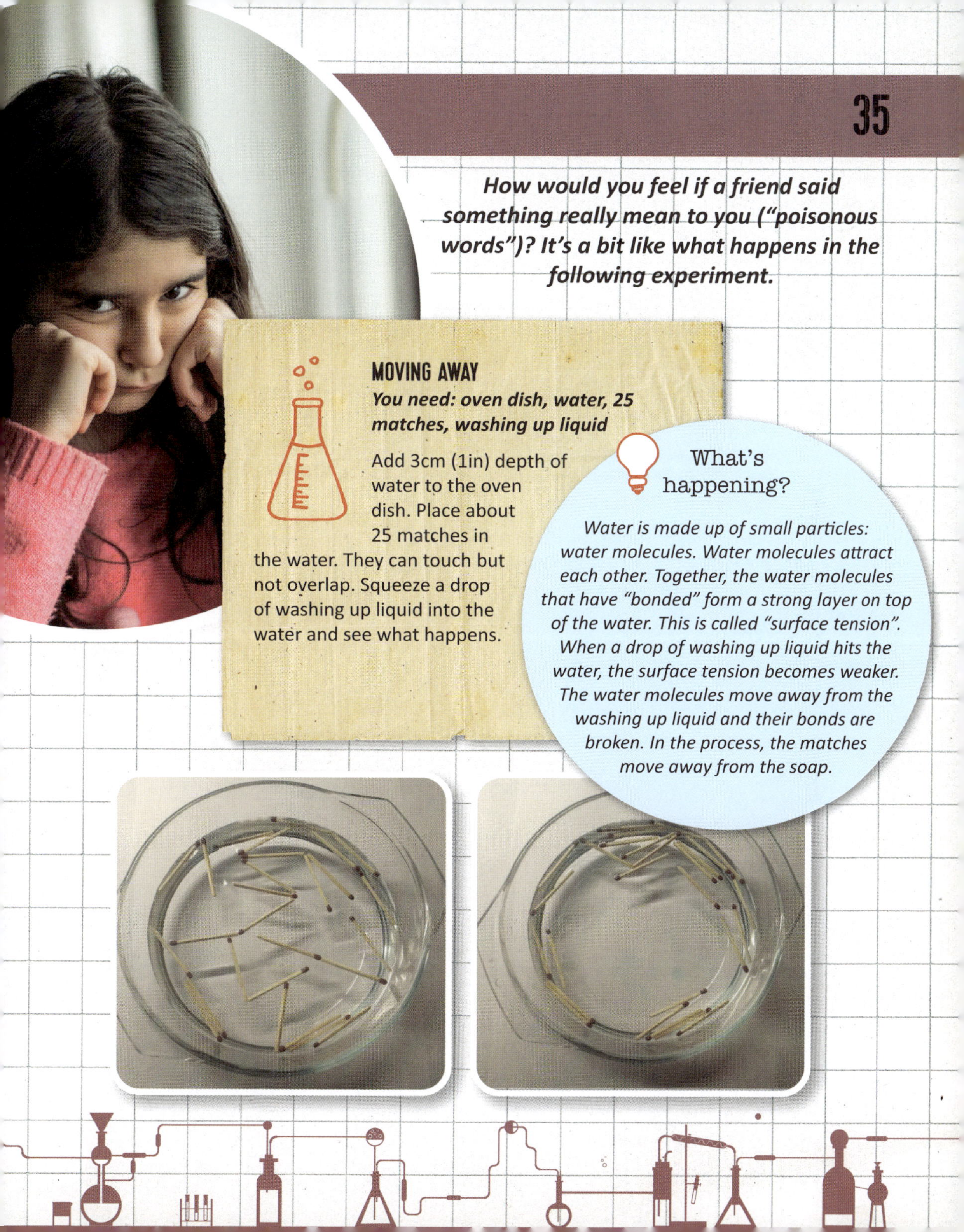

How would you feel if a friend said something really mean to you ("poisonous words")? It's a bit like what happens in the following experiment.

MOVING AWAY

You need: oven dish, water, 25 matches, washing up liquid

Add 3cm (1in) depth of water to the oven dish. Place about 25 matches in the water. They can touch but not overlap. Squeeze a drop of washing up liquid into the water and see what happens.

What's happening?

Water is made up of small particles: water molecules. Water molecules attract each other. Together, the water molecules that have "bonded" form a strong layer on top of the water. This is called "surface tension". When a drop of washing up liquid hits the water, the surface tension becomes weaker. The water molecules move away from the washing up liquid and their bonds are broken. In the process, the matches move away from the soap.

THE POWER OF SOUND

Jericho's walls JOSHUA 6

Read the story in the Bible (Joshua 2 and 6:6–23).

On the seventh day, they got up at day-break and marched round the city seven times in the same manner, except that on that day they circled the city seven times. The seventh time round, when the priests sounded the trumpet blast, Joshua commanded the army, "Shout! For the Lord has given you the city!"
Joshua 6:15–16

USE SOUND TO BLOW DOWN DOMINOES

You need: plastic bucket (not too precious, as it will be cut), knife, plastic carrier bag, dominoes, tape

Ask an adult to cut out a hole in the bottom of the bucket the size of a CD. Stretch the carrier bag across the top of the bucket and firmly attach to the bucket with tape. Make sure the plastic is stretched tightly across like drum skin. When you tap the plastic, you don't just hear the sound, but you also feel air coming out of the hole in the bottom of the bucket.

Build a line of dominoes. Position the bucket with the hole pointing towards the first tile. Hit the plastic (on the top of the bucket). Can you "knock down" the first tile with the banging on your bucket drum?

ASK AN ADULT TO HELP YOU.

What's happening?

Sound is made when something starts to vibrate. These vibrations are called sound waves. Sound waves also cause other things to vibrate. Place your hand on a speaker and play music with a heavy bass. Can you feel the vibrations? Do you think the sound of an old-fashioned trumpet (made from the horn of a ram) was powerful enough to make the walls of Jericho collapse? No, this was a real miracle!

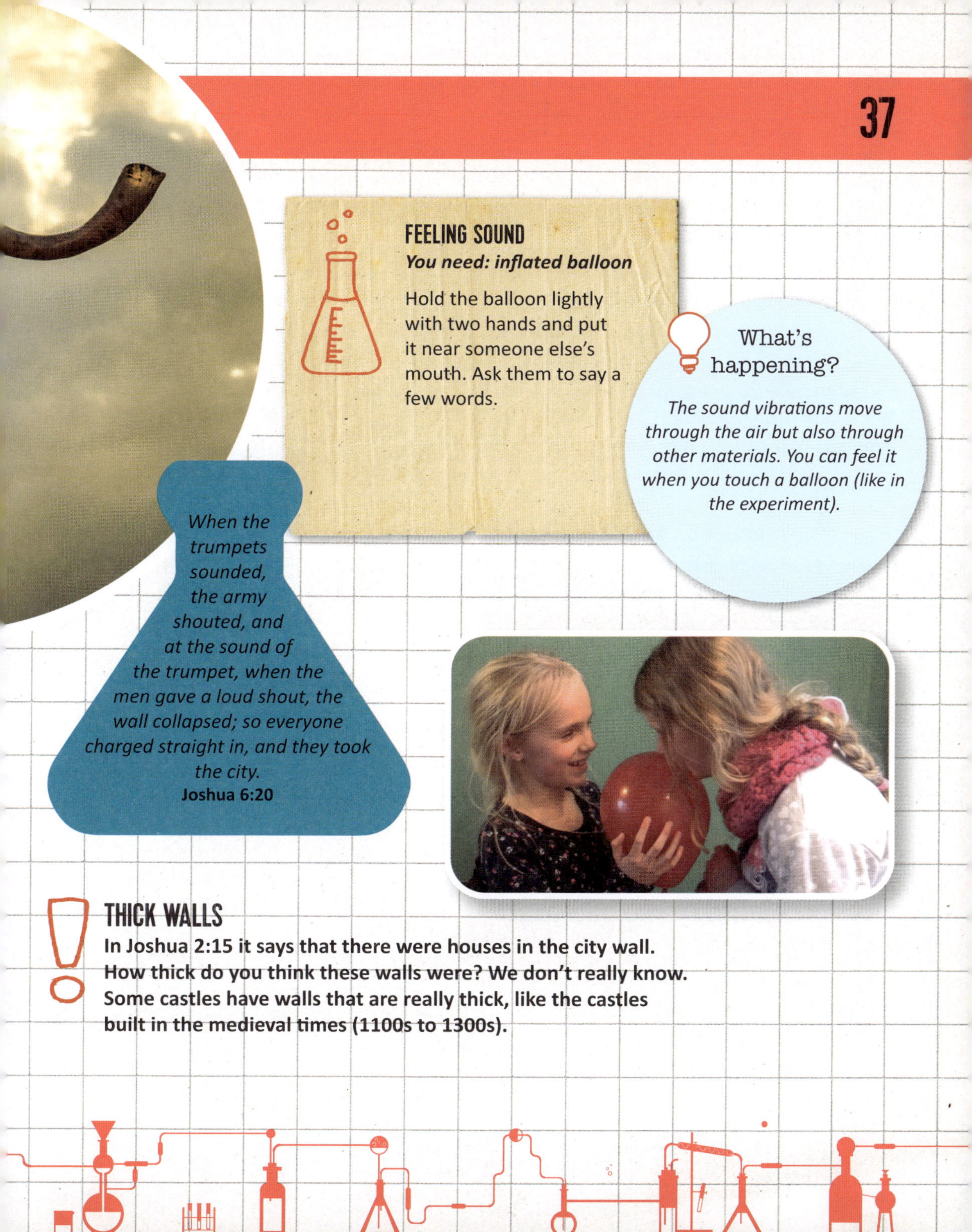

FEELING SOUND

You need: inflated balloon

Hold the balloon lightly with two hands and put it near someone else's mouth. Ask them to say a few words.

What's happening?

The sound vibrations move through the air but also through other materials. You can feel it when you touch a balloon (like in the experiment).

When the trumpets sounded, the army shouted, and at the sound of the trumpet, when the men gave a loud shout, the wall collapsed; so everyone charged straight in, and they took the city.
Joshua 6:20

THICK WALLS

In Joshua 2:15 it says that there were houses in the city wall. How thick do you think these walls were? We don't really know. Some castles have walls that are really thick, like the castles built in the medieval times (1100s to 1300s).

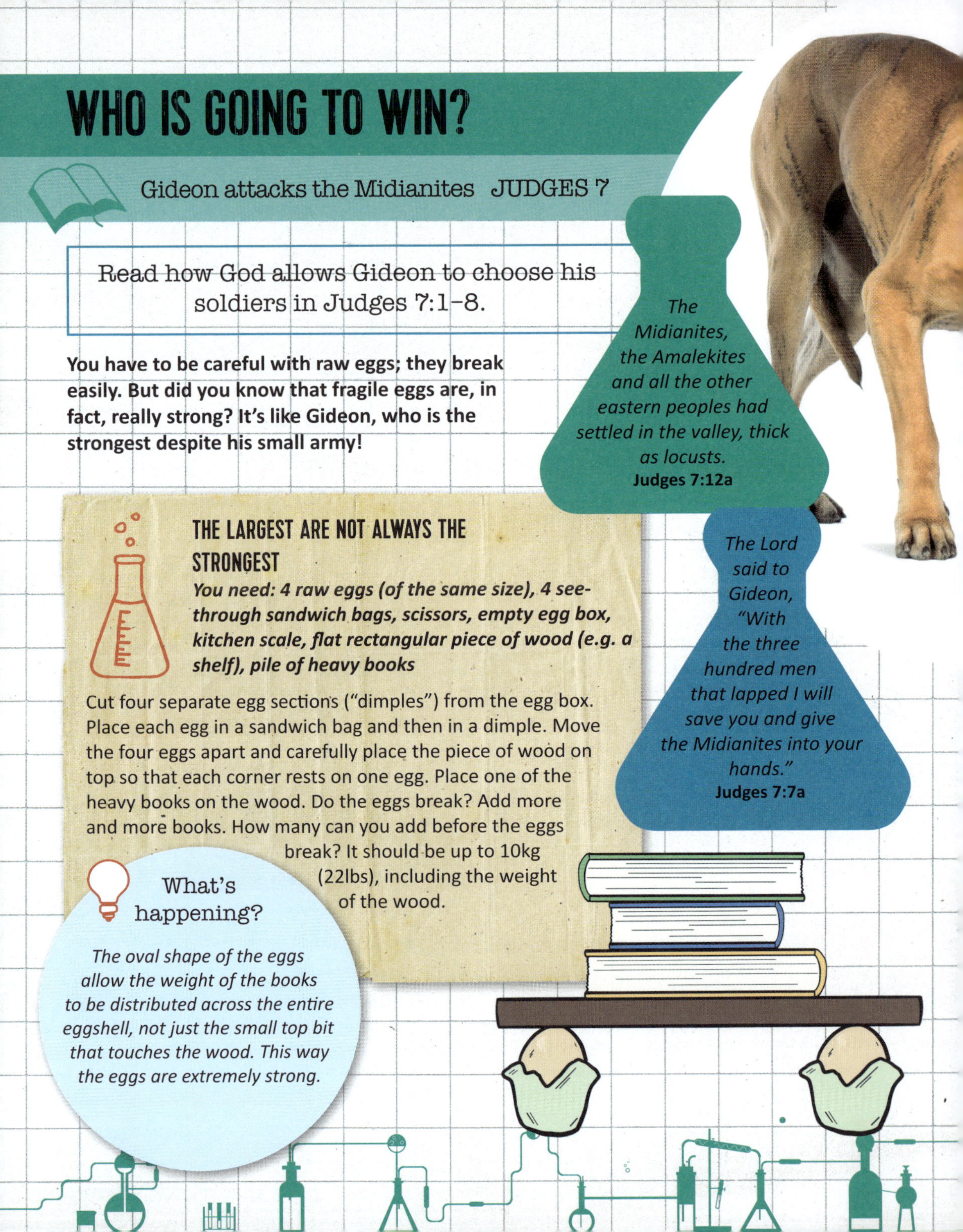

WHO IS GOING TO WIN?

Gideon attacks the Midianites JUDGES 7

Read how God allows Gideon to choose his soldiers in Judges 7:1–8.

You have to be careful with raw eggs; they break easily. But did you know that fragile eggs are, in fact, really strong? It's like Gideon, who is the strongest despite his small army!

The Midianites, the Amalekites and all the other eastern peoples had settled in the valley, thick as locusts.
Judges 7:12a

THE LARGEST ARE NOT ALWAYS THE STRONGEST

You need: 4 raw eggs (of the same size), 4 see-through sandwich bags, scissors, empty egg box, kitchen scale, flat rectangular piece of wood (e.g. a shelf), pile of heavy books

Cut four separate egg sections ("dimples") from the egg box. Place each egg in a sandwich bag and then in a dimple. Move the four eggs apart and carefully place the piece of wood on top so that each corner rests on one egg. Place one of the heavy books on the wood. Do the eggs break? Add more and more books. How many can you add before the eggs break? It should be up to 10kg (22lbs), including the weight of the wood.

The Lord said to Gideon, "With the three hundred men that lapped I will save you and give the Midianites into your hands."
Judges 7:7a

What's happening?

The oval shape of the eggs allow the weight of the books to be distributed across the entire eggshell, not just the small top bit that touches the wood. This way the eggs are extremely strong.

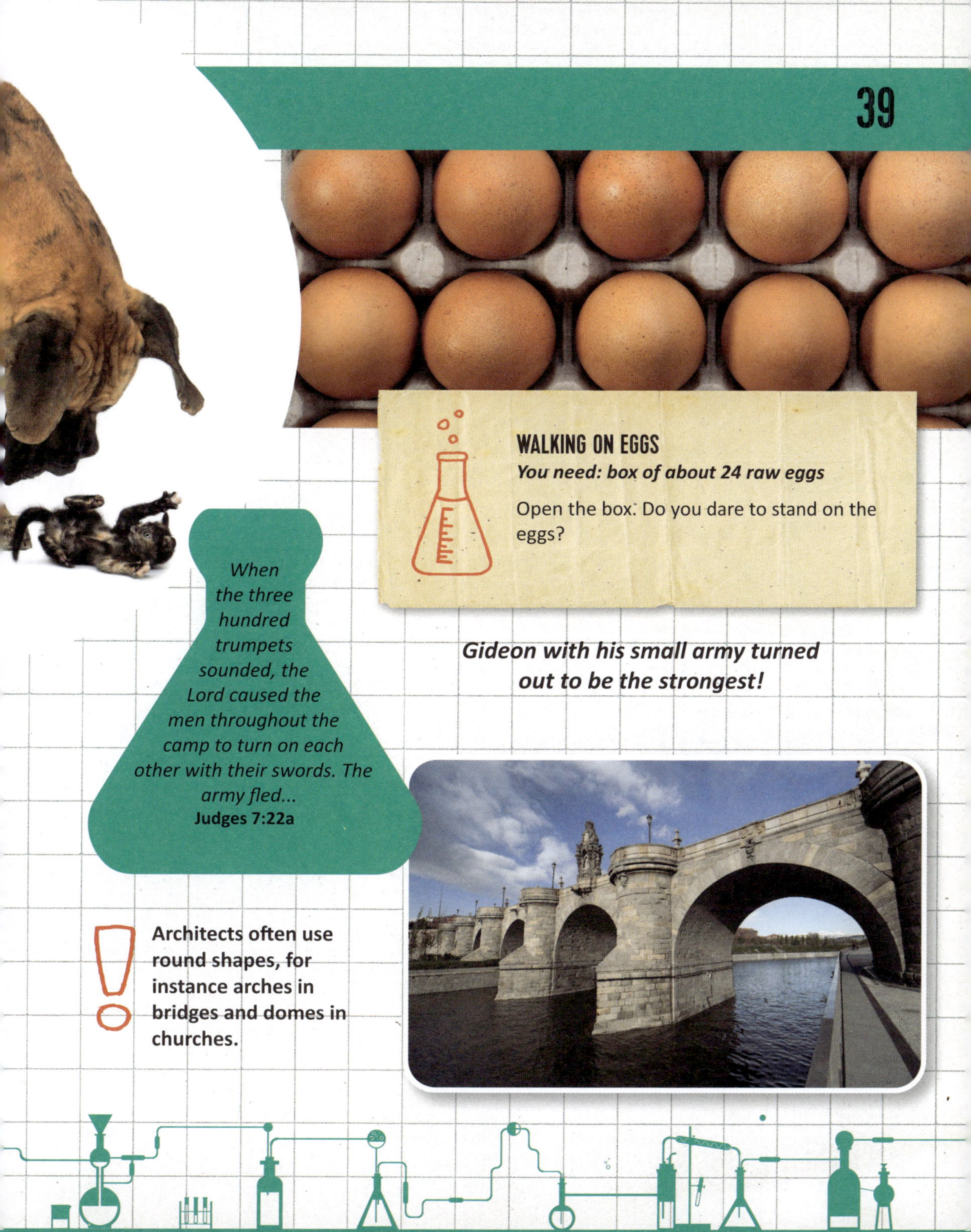

WALKING ON EGGS

You need: box of about 24 raw eggs

Open the box. Do you dare to stand on the eggs?

Gideon with his small army turned out to be the strongest!

When the three hundred trumpets sounded, the Lord caused the men throughout the camp to turn on each other with their swords. The army fled...
Judges 7:22a

Architects often use round shapes, for instance arches in bridges and domes in churches.

GROWING BY INVISIBLE POWER

David and Goliath 1 SAMUEL 17

Read the story of David and Goliath in 1 Samuel 17.

David said to the Philistine, "You come against me with sword and spear and javelin, but I come against you in the name of the Lord Almighty, the God of the armies of Israel, whom you have defied."
1 Samuel 17:45

ASK AN ADULT TO HELP YOU.

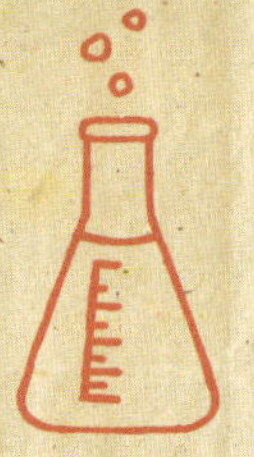

INVISIBLE POWER

You need: microwave, microwaveable plate, marshmallows, ruler

Measure the marshmallow. How long is it?
Place the marshmallow in the middle of the plate.
Put the plate in the microwave and heat up for 30 seconds. Keep watching!
What happens after about 15 seconds? Remove the plate from the microwave after 30 seconds. Watch out! The marshmallow is hot. How big is it now?

Tip: You could put a bar of soap in the microwave. What happens to the soap?

"All those gathered here will know that it is not by sword or spear that the Lord saves; for the battle is the Lord's, and he will give all of you into our hands."
1 Samuel 17:47

What's happening?

Food is heated up in a microwave thanks to "microwaves". There are tiny air bubbles in marshmallows, which contain molecules. When a marshmallow heats up, these molecules start to move more quickly. Because of this frantic movement, the pressure within the air bubbles increases and each bubble puffs up, like a blown up balloon.

David trusts in God

WHAT IS TRUST?

You need two people for this. The first person stands up straight with their back to the second person. When the second person is ready, the first person falls back and the second person catches them. Do you trust the catcher?

HOW DOES A MICROWAVE WORK?

In a microwave there is a tube that conducts (passes on) electricity and is surrounded by magnets. The electricity is pushed along at top speed and this creates microwaves. These waves make sure that the molecules in your food start to "vibrate" and collide with each other. This creates friction (a force between two sliding surfaces) and friction creates heat. This way, the food in the microwave heats up.

Would you like to feel how friction works? Rub your hands for ten seconds and feel the heat you create.

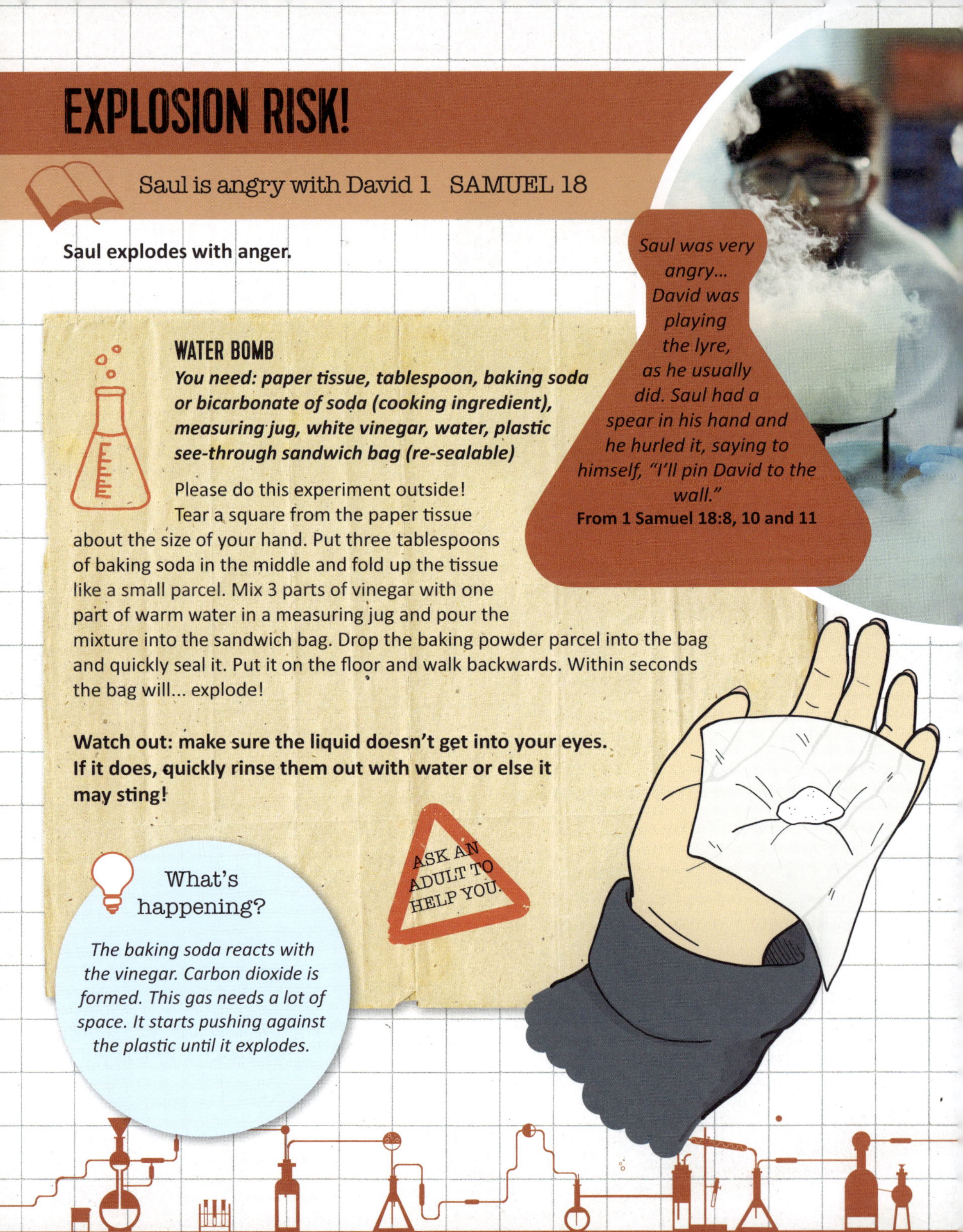

EXPLOSION RISK!

Saul is angry with David 1 SAMUEL 18

Saul explodes with anger.

Saul was very angry... David was playing the lyre, as he usually did. Saul had a spear in his hand and he hurled it, saying to himself, "I'll pin David to the wall."

From 1 Samuel 18:8, 10 and 11

WATER BOMB

You need: paper tissue, tablespoon, baking soda or bicarbonate of soda (cooking ingredient), measuring jug, white vinegar, water, plastic see-through sandwich bag (re-sealable)

Please do this experiment outside!

Tear a square from the paper tissue about the size of your hand. Put three tablespoons of baking soda in the middle and fold up the tissue like a small parcel. Mix 3 parts of vinegar with one part of warm water in a measuring jug and pour the mixture into the sandwich bag. Drop the baking powder parcel into the bag and quickly seal it. Put it on the floor and walk backwards. Within seconds the bag will... explode!

Watch out: make sure the liquid doesn't get into your eyes. If it does, quickly rinse them out with water or else it may sting!

ASK AN ADULT TO HELP YOU.

What's happening?

The baking soda reacts with the vinegar. Carbon dioxide is formed. This gas needs a lot of space. It starts pushing against the plastic until it explodes.

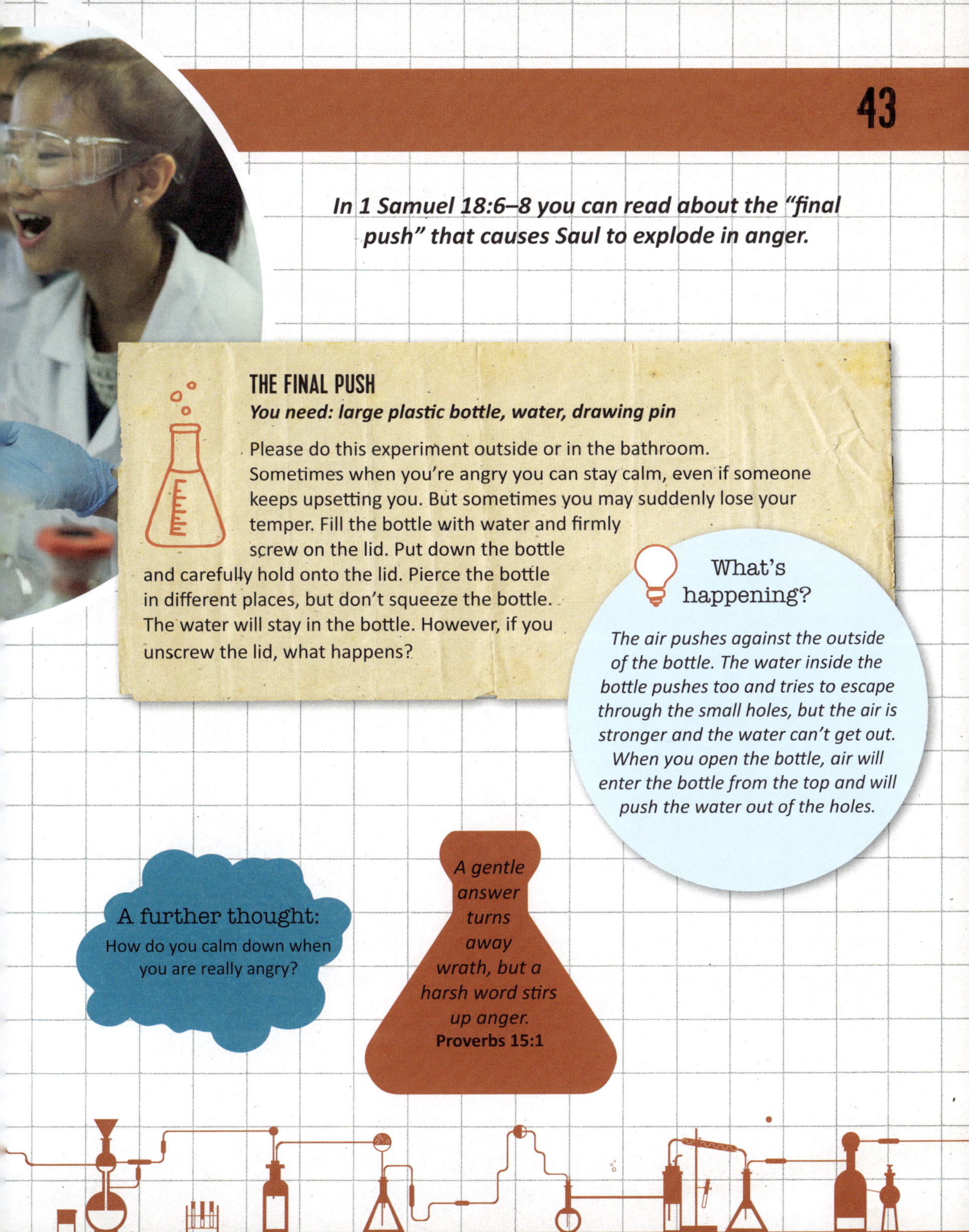

In 1 Samuel 18:6–8 you can read about the "final push" that causes Saul to explode in anger.

THE FINAL PUSH

You need: large plastic bottle, water, drawing pin

Please do this experiment outside or in the bathroom. Sometimes when you're angry you can stay calm, even if someone keeps upsetting you. But sometimes you may suddenly lose your temper. Fill the bottle with water and firmly screw on the lid. Put down the bottle and carefully hold onto the lid. Pierce the bottle in different places, but don't squeeze the bottle. The water will stay in the bottle. However, if you unscrew the lid, what happens?

What's happening?

The air pushes against the outside of the bottle. The water inside the bottle pushes too and tries to escape through the small holes, but the air is stronger and the water can't get out. When you open the bottle, air will enter the bottle from the top and will push the water out of the holes.

A further thought:

How do you calm down when you are really angry?

A gentle answer turns away wrath, but a harsh word stirs up anger.
Proverbs 15:1

AHIJAH'S CLOAK

The land of Israel is being divided 1 KINGS 11

God divides the land of Israel and its tribes.

DIVISION

You need: 26 matches

Create the figure below with the 26 matches. Take away ten matches so two separate, closed shapes remain: a big one and a small one.

Tip: Find the solution on page 142.

About that time Jeroboam was going out of Jerusalem, and Ahijah the prophet of Shiloh met him on the way, wearing a new cloak. The two of them were alone out in the country, and Ahijah took hold of the new cloak he was wearing and tore it into twelve pieces. Then he said to Jeroboam, "Take ten pieces for yourself, for this is what the Lord, the God of Israel, says: 'See, I am going to tear the kingdom out of Solomon's hand and give you ten tribes.'"

1 Kings 11:29–31

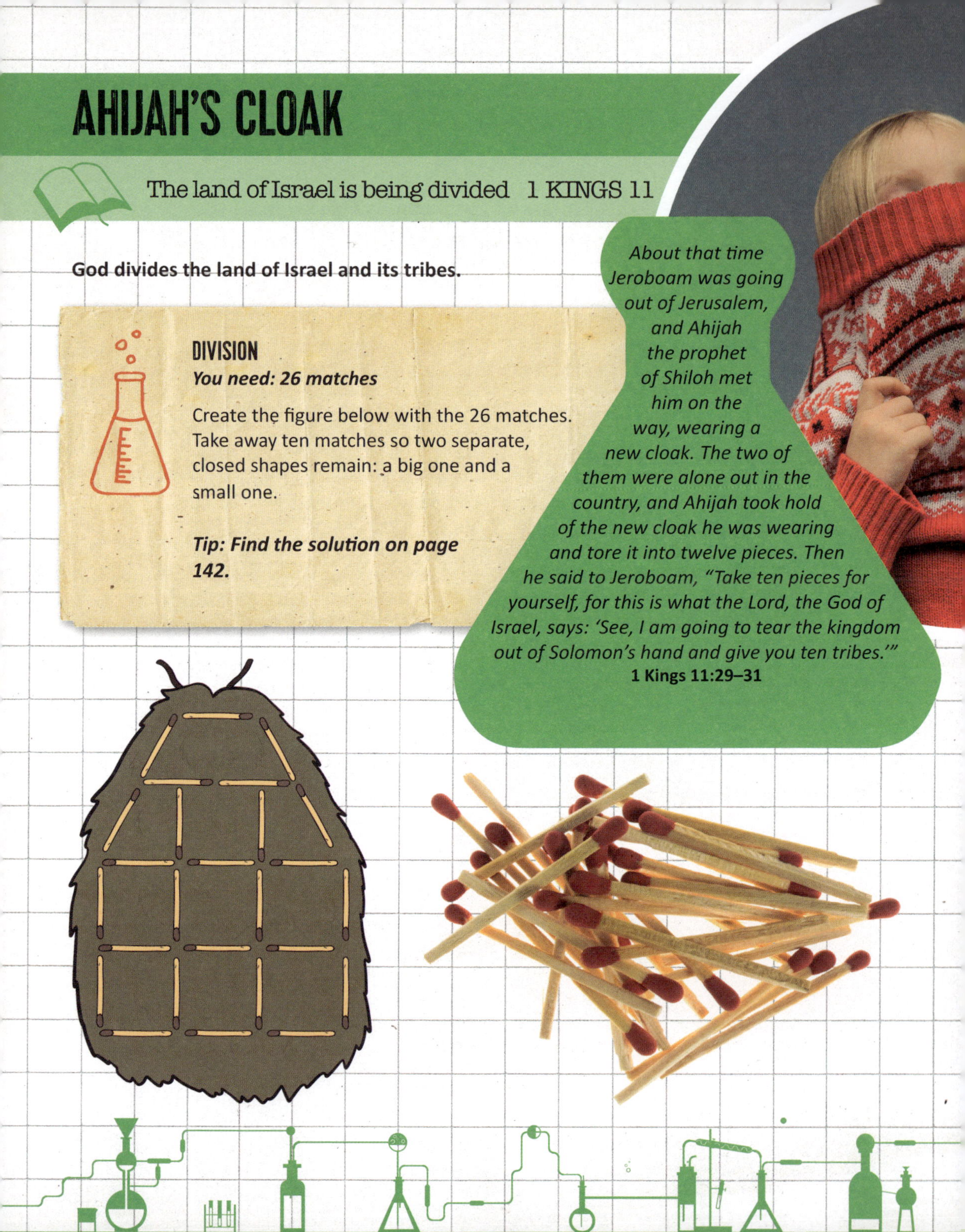

SEPARATION

You need: coarse salt, pepper and pepper mill, plastic spoon, wool or woollen jumper

Sprinkle some coarse salt on the table and mix with some freshly ground pepper. How are you going to separate the two again? Rub the plastic spoon with the wool. Hold the plastic spoon over the pepper and salt and lower very gently. What happens next?

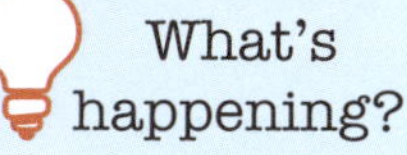

Rubbing a plastic spoon on woollen material electrically charges the spoon. If you move the spoon toward the pepper (not too close), the pepper will be lifted off the surface by the electricity. Pepper is light, but the salt will lift as well once you have lowered the spoon a bit more.

PEPPER MAKES YOU SNEEZE, HOW IS THAT POSSIBLE?

Your nose is a kind of filter. It filters out all dirt from the air you breath in. That's why there are small hairs in your nose. These hairs prevent the dirt from entering your lungs. However, very small dirt particles like pepper get through and end up in the mucous membrane behind the hairs. When this happens, you have to sneeze. Your lungs press together to squeeze out the air inside at 150 km (93 miles) per hour. In the process, everything inside your nose flies out too.

A GOOD KING OR...

Wise counsel for Rehoboam 1 KINGS 12

Rehoboam is about to become king. On behalf of the Israelites, Jeroboam asks him the following: ⇨

"Your father put a heavy yoke on us, but now lighten the harsh labour and the heavy yoke he put on us, and we will serve you."
1 Kings 12:4

Rehoboam seeks advice. First he asks his father's counsellors. They say: ⇨

"If today you will be a servant to these people and serve them and give them a favourable answer, they will always be your servants."
1 Kings 12:7

POSITIVE INFLUENCE

You need: glass of water, ink (for instance from a fountain pen refill)

If you do something well, if you help someone or act kindly, something happens to other people around you. You can compare this with a drop of ink in a glass of water. Squeeze a drop of ink into the glass of water. What can you see? Leave the glass of water for a bit. What happens to the water?

Rehoboam also asks the young men he grew up with for their advice. They say: ⇦

"Now tell them, 'My little finger is thicker than my father's waist. My father laid on you a heavy yoke; I will make it even heavier. My father scourged you with whips; I will scourge you with scorpions.'"
1 Kings 12:10–11

What's happening?

The drop of ink falls through the air until it hits the water. It crashes into the water particles and the ink drop falls apart and the smaller droplets move down. The droplets leave a trail of colour. After a while, the ink mixes with the water and the colour of the water is the same everywhere.

The following experiment will show you what Rehoboam is planning to do with the people of Israel: exploit and crush them, so he can take advantage.

ASK AN ADULT TO HELP YOU.

SQUEEZING AND CRUSHING

You need: empty drinks can, hot plate (to keep food or drinks warm), large pliers or barbecue tongs, water, a large (washing up) bowl of cold water

Pour 1cm (⅓in) of water into the can. Place the can on the hot plate. Heat up until you can see steam coming out of the can opening. Keep on boiling until the can is filled with water vapour. Pick up the can with the tongs or pliers and plunge upside down into the bowl of cold water.

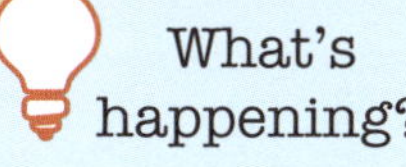

What's happening?

When water boils it becomes water vapour (steam). It pushes the air out of the can. Water becomes vapour above 100°C (212°F). When you immerse the can in cold water, the temperature drops quickly to about 80°C (176°F). The vapour turns into water drops, which take up less space than vapour and so the pressure in the can drops. There is nothing left inside the can that is pushing against the inside walls, but on the outside, air is pushing against the can and crushes it.

The dictionary says that to "exploit" means to "benefit unfairly from the work of someone, typically by overworking or underpaying them."

Rehoboam has to choose. Do you want to know how it ends? Read 1 Kings 12:16, 17 and 20.

LIKE A BURNING FIRE

Elijah brings a sacrifice on Mount Carmel 1 KINGS 18

The prophets of Baal (a pagan god) and the prophet Elijah are on Mount Carmel to bring a sacrifice, each to their own god. It's almost like a competition! Which god will light the sacrifice? Baal or the God of Elijah?

Midday passed, and they continued their frantic prophesying until the time for the evening sacrifice. But there was no response, no one answered, no one paid attention.
1 Kings 18:29

WHAT DOES A FIRE NEED TO BURN?

You need: 2 small plates, 2 tea lights, lighter, glass, cup of water

Place a tea light on each plate. Pour water on one of the lights, so it's soaking wet. Try to light both tea lights. Is it possible? Place the glass over the burning tea light (upside down). What happens next?

ASK AN ADULT TO HELP YOU.

Then he said to them, "Fill four large jars with water and pour it on the offering and on the wood." "Do it again," he said, and they did it again. "Do it a third time," he ordered, and they did it the third time. The water ran down around the altar and even filled the trench.
1 Kings 18:33b – 35

What's happening?

The air is made up of oxygen, a gas. Humans and animals need oxygen to survive. That's why we breathe in air! To light a fire and keep it going three things are needed: fuel (like wood or wax), heat and oxygen. If one of those is lacking, the fire won't start or it will stop burning.

The prophet Elijah stepped forward and prayed: "Lord, the God of Abraham, Isaac and Israel, let it be known today that you are God in Israel and that I am your servant and have done all these things at your command." Then the fire of the Lord fell and burned up the sacrifice, the wood, the stones and the soil, and also licked up the water in the trench.
1 Kings 18:36 and 38

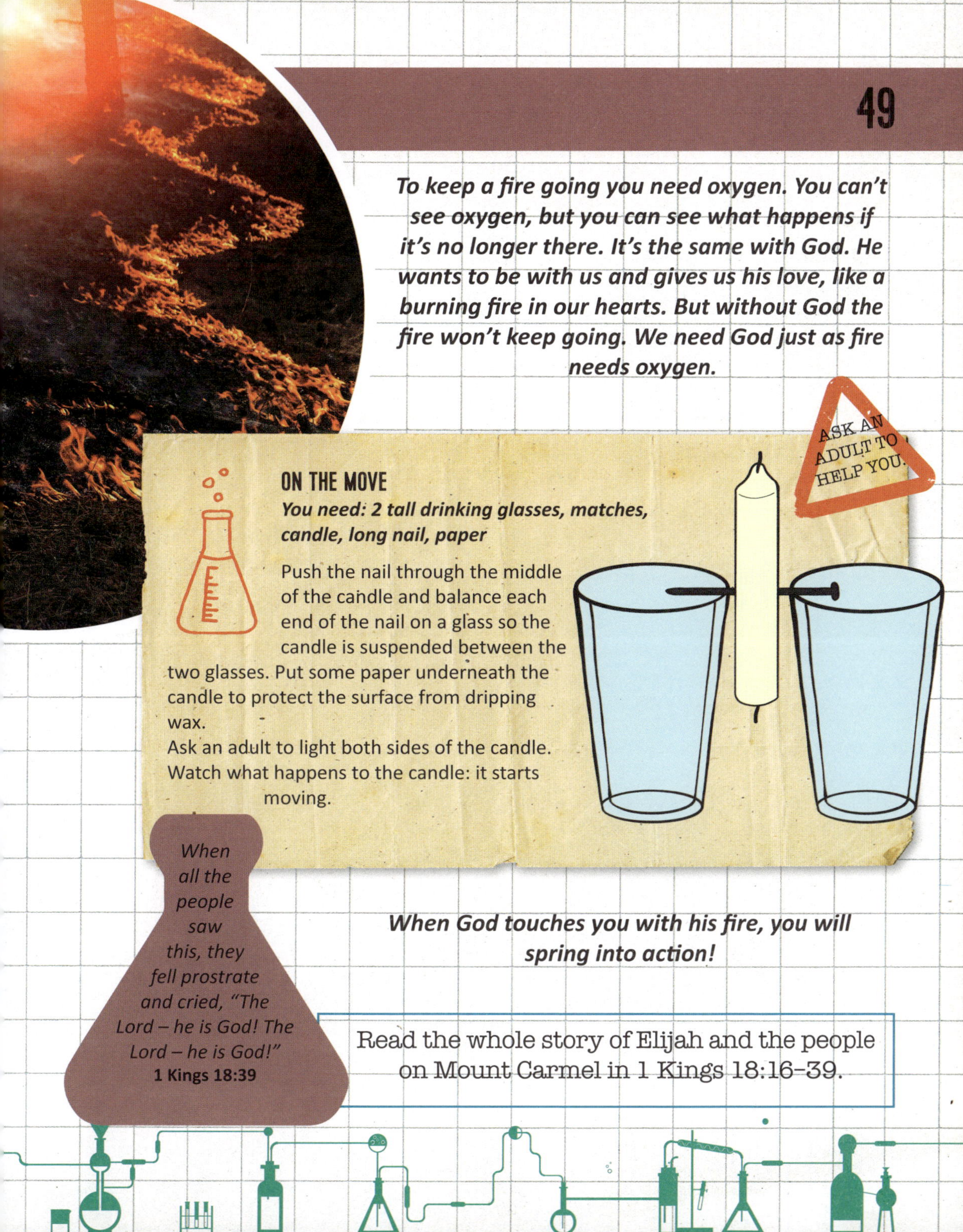

To keep a fire going you need oxygen. You can't see oxygen, but you can see what happens if it's no longer there. It's the same with God. He wants to be with us and gives us his love, like a burning fire in our hearts. But without God the fire won't keep going. We need God just as fire needs oxygen.

ON THE MOVE

You need: 2 tall drinking glasses, matches, candle, long nail, paper

Push the nail through the middle of the candle and balance each end of the nail on a glass so the candle is suspended between the two glasses. Put some paper underneath the candle to protect the surface from dripping wax.

Ask an adult to light both sides of the candle. Watch what happens to the candle: it starts moving.

When all the people saw this, they fell prostrate and cried, "The Lord – he is God! The Lord – he is God!"
1 Kings 18:39

When God touches you with his fire, you will spring into action!

Read the whole story of Elijah and the people on Mount Carmel in 1 Kings 18:16–39.

THE POWER OF PRAYER

Elijah prays for rain 1 KINGS 18 AND JAMES 5

Prayer is talking with God. God listens and responds.

Read how Elijah prays for rain in 1 Kings 18:41–45.

Is anyone among you in trouble? Let them pray. Is anyone happy? Let them sing songs of praise... Therefore confess your sins to each other and pray for each other so that you may be healed. The prayer of a righteous person is powerful and effective. Elijah was a human being, even as we are. He prayed earnestly that it would not rain, and it did not rain on the land for three and a half years. Again he prayed, and the heavens gave rain, and the earth produced its crops.
James 5:13 and 16–18

THE LIGHT GOES ON

You need: energy-saving light bulb, balloon, dry hair

When you pray in silence you "think" words. Does anything happen to those words?

Blow up the balloon and tie a knot in it. Go into a dark room and rub the balloon on your hair. Put the light bulb against the balloon.

A further thought:

"If you believe, you will receive whatever you ask for in prayer."
Matthew 21:22

When you talk to God, ask him questions or say a prayer (in your head or out loud) something really happens. God is like the invisible power that makes the light bulb in the experiment glow.

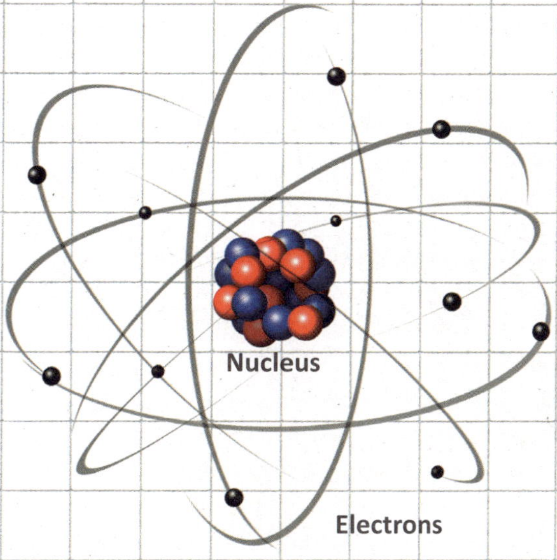

Nucleus

Electrons

What's happening?

You and everything around you is made up of molecules. Atoms make up molecules. An atom consists of a core (nucleus) surrounded by electrons. The electrons spin around the nucleus at top speed. If you rub a balloon on your hair, electrons jump from your hair onto the balloon and "charge" the balloon. This is called "static electricity". When you put the light bulb against the balloon, the balloon will be able to get rid of its charge of static electricity. It passes it to the bulb which will start glowing.

Molecules are tiny. If you lined up enough molecules to make one millimetre, you would need one million of them! Atoms and electrons are even smaller.

IN A CHARIOT OF FIRE

Elijah goes up to heaven 2 KINGS 2

Read the whole story in 2 Kings 2:7–18.

As they were walking along and talking together, suddenly a chariot of fire and horses of fire appeared and separated the two of them, and Elijah went up to heaven in a whirl-wind.
2 Kings 2:11

FIRE THAT GOES UP

You need: pyramid shaped teabag (paper, not plastic), matches or lighter, scissors

Cut off the top (and any labels/string) of the tea bag (with a wider bit at the bottom so it can stand up unaided when empty) and shake out the tea. Open up the empty bag and stand it upright. Ask an adult to light the top.

Tip: Do this experiment on a kitchen surface.

ASK AN ADULT TO HELP YOU.

What's happening?

The air in and around the teabag warms up when lit. Warm air rises and is so strong that it lifts up the empty teabag too.

The story about Elijah who ascends to heaven is a special story. You can draw what happened and look at each other's artwork.

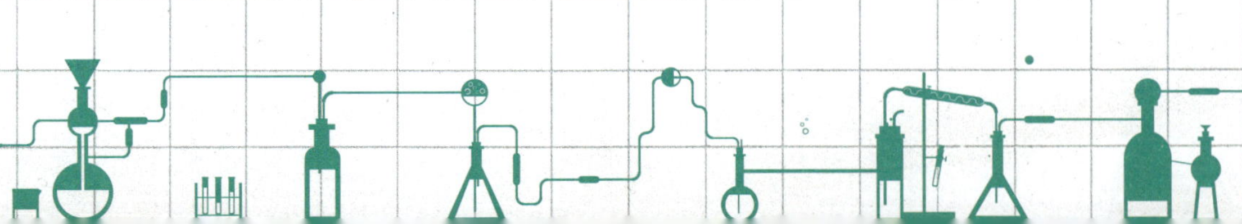

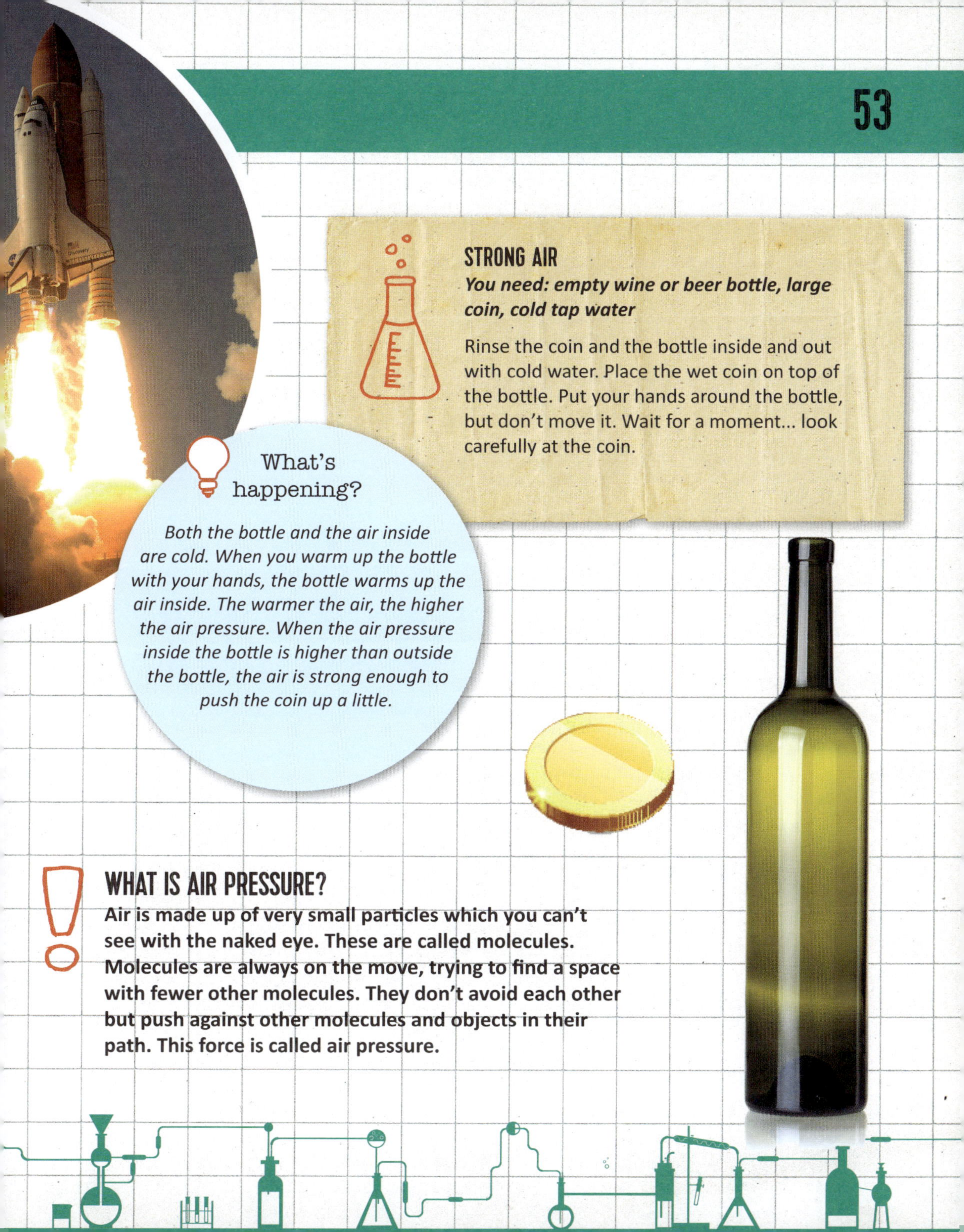

STRONG AIR

You need: empty wine or beer bottle, large coin, cold tap water

Rinse the coin and the bottle inside and out with cold water. Place the wet coin on top of the bottle. Put your hands around the bottle, but don't move it. Wait for a moment... look carefully at the coin.

What's happening?

Both the bottle and the air inside are cold. When you warm up the bottle with your hands, the bottle warms up the air inside. The warmer the air, the higher the air pressure. When the air pressure inside the bottle is higher than outside the bottle, the air is strong enough to push the coin up a little.

WHAT IS AIR PRESSURE?

Air is made up of very small particles which you can't see with the naked eye. These are called molecules. Molecules are always on the move, trying to find a space with fewer other molecules. They don't avoid each other but push against other molecules and objects in their path. This force is called air pressure.

WASHED CLEAN

The healing of Naaman 2 KINGS 5

Naaman suffers from leprosy. He is covered in ulcers. He's hoping that the prophet Elisha will heal him.

Read the whole story in 2 Kings 5.

So Naaman went with his horses and chariots and stopped at the door of Elisha's house. Elisha sent a messenger to say to him, "Go, wash yourself seven times in the Jordan, and your flesh will be restored and you will be cleansed."
2 Kings 5:9–10

COMPLETELY CLEAN

You need: copper coin, glass, lemon juice, egg timer

Squeeze a layer of lemon juice into the glass. Add the coin. Set the egg timer for five minutes. When the time has passed, lift the coin out. Doesn't it look sparkling clean?

What's happening?

The coin is made of copper-plated steel, which over time reacts with the oxygen in the air forming a dark layer (copper oxide). The acid in the lemon juice dissolves this layer and after five minutes the coin looks like new again.

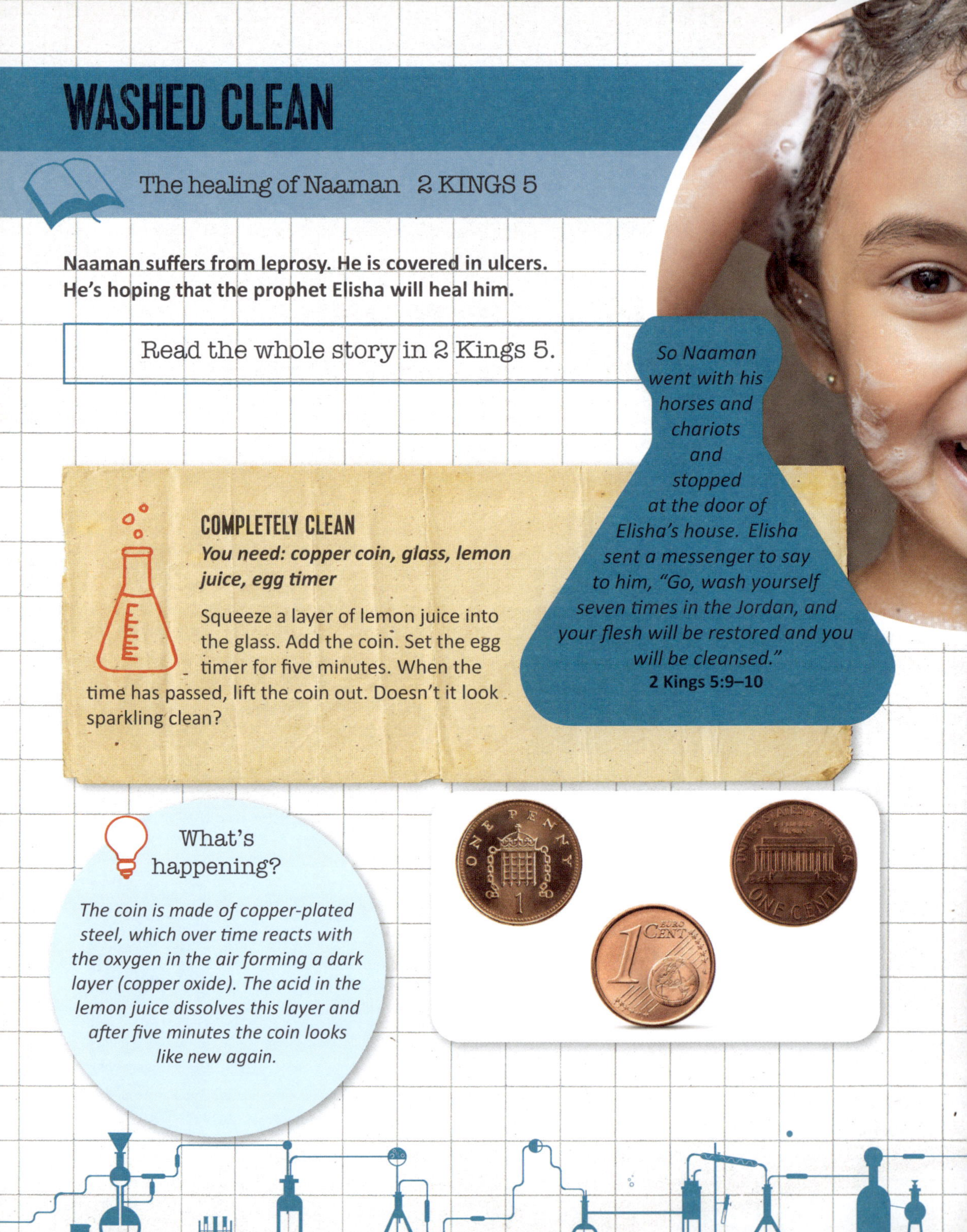

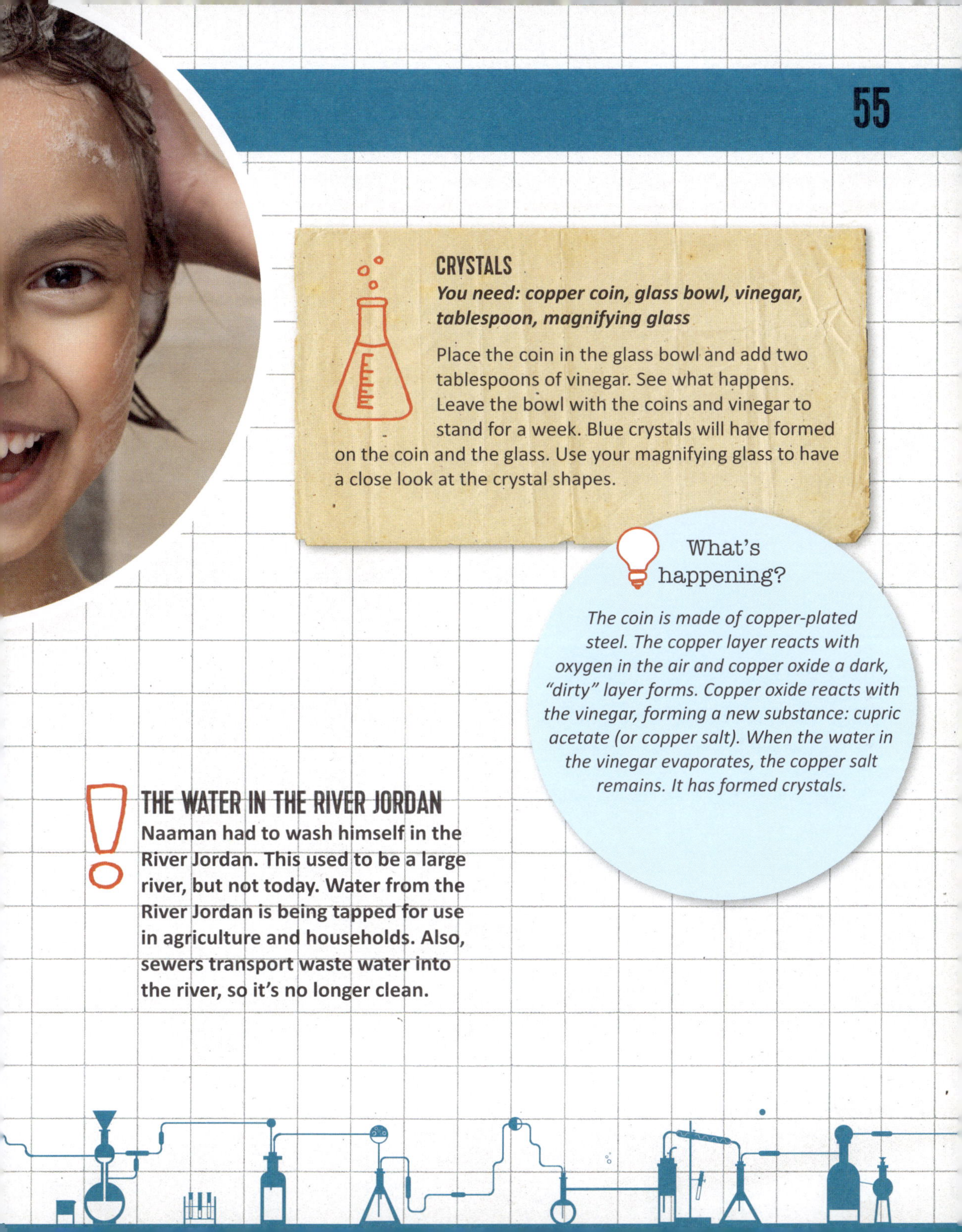

CRYSTALS

You need: copper coin, glass bowl, vinegar, tablespoon, magnifying glass

Place the coin in the glass bowl and add two tablespoons of vinegar. See what happens. Leave the bowl with the coins and vinegar to stand for a week. Blue crystals will have formed on the coin and the glass. Use your magnifying glass to have a close look at the crystal shapes.

What's happening?

The coin is made of copper-plated steel. The copper layer reacts with oxygen in the air and copper oxide a dark, "dirty" layer forms. Copper oxide reacts with the vinegar, forming a new substance: cupric acetate (or copper salt). When the water in the vinegar evaporates, the copper salt remains. It has formed crystals.

THE WATER IN THE RIVER JORDAN

Naaman had to wash himself in the River Jordan. This used to be a large river, but not today. Water from the River Jordan is being tapped for use in agriculture and households. Also, sewers transport waste water into the river, so it's no longer clean.

DOES THE EARTH ROTATE AROUND THE SUN...

A sign for Hezekiah 2 KINGS 20

King Hezekiah is ill and he's desperate! The prophet Isaiah promises him that God will heal him.

Isaiah answered, "This is the Lord's sign to you that the Lord will do what he has promised: shall the shadow go forward ten steps, or shall it go back ten steps?"
"It is a simple matter for the shadow to go forward ten steps," said Hezekiah. "Rather, let it go back ten steps." Then the prophet Isaiah called on the Lord, and the Lord made the shadow go back the ten steps it had gone down on the stairway of Ahaz.
2 Kings 20:9–11

THE SUN, THE EARTH, AND THE MOON

You need: white card, pair of compasses, scissors, pens or pencils, 3 split pins

Draw three circles on the white card (see below). Cut out the circles and colour them in: yellow (the sun), blue and green (the earth), and the moon (light grey with dark grey spots).

Cut out two strips of white card, one measuring 20 x 2.5cm (7⅔ x 1in) and one 12 x 2.5cm (4⅔ x 1in). Attach one end of the short strip to the moon using a split pin. Attach the earth to the other side of the strip. Use the same split pin to attach one end of the long strip and add the sun to the other end. Your model is ready. The earth rotates around the sun. The moon rotates around the earth. Try this out using your model.

COPERNICUS AND GALILEO

In the past people thought that the sun, just like the moon, rotated around the earth. The German scientist Nicholas Copernicus was the first to claim that the earth rotates around the sun. But a lot of people didn't agree! The sixteenth century astronomer Galileo Galilei improved the telescope. He was able to develop Copernicus' ideas further. However, the church believed these ideas were in conflict with the Bible. They condemned his books and forbade people to read them. Galileo ended up under house arrest for nine years!

Tip: Read Joshua 10:12. Can you understand how people believed that the sun rotated around the earth?

SOLAR ECLIPSE

Can you create a solar eclipse out of the model you made earlier? This is when the moon blocks the sun's light.

MAKE A SUNDIAL

You need: white card, pair of compasses, scissors, nail, pen, small stick, ruler, clock

Use the pair of compasses to draw a circle with a diameter of 20cm (7⅘in) on the card and cut out the circle. Pierce a hole in the middle with the nail and push the stick through. Go outside and place the stick upright into the soil in a sunny spot, and push the circle down flat onto the ground. Go out every hour and draw the shadow on the card. Start in the middle and draw a line to the outside of the circle with a ruler. Note down the time of day on the line. After one day your sundial is ready. From now on you can tell the time by looking at the shadow of the stick on the card.

It was now about noon, and darkness came over the whole land until three in the afternoon, for the sun stopped shining. And the curtain of the temple was torn in two. Jesus called out with a loud voice, "Father, into your hands I commit my spirit." When he had said this, he breathed his last.

Luke 23:44–46

BATTERED AND BRUISED (1)

Job's adversity JOB 3

If someone from the Bible is known for their setbacks, it's Job, a good and honest man. He loses everything and sits desperate and lonely in a heap of ash.

"Why is life given to a man whose way is hidden, whom God has hedged in? I have no peace, no quietness; I have no rest, but only turmoil."
Job 3:23 and 26

BATTERED AND BRUISED

You need: 3 plastic cups, 2 sheets of A4

Place two plastic cups on a surface, leaving a bit of space between them. Place an A4 sheet on top. Place a third cup on top. Does it stay? Fold the other piece of paper in a zigzag. Place this piece on top of the cups and put the third cup on top of the paper. What happens – does it stay?

God makes you strong, even if you are battered and bruised. Sometimes you're even stronger because of the setbacks.

He gives strength to the weary and increases the power of the weak. Even youths grow tired and weary, and young men stumble and fall; but those who hope in the Lord will renew their strength.
Isaiah 40:29–31a

A further thought:

Because you know that the testing of your faith produces perseverance. Let perseverance finish its work so that you may be mature and complete, not lacking anything.
James 1:3–4

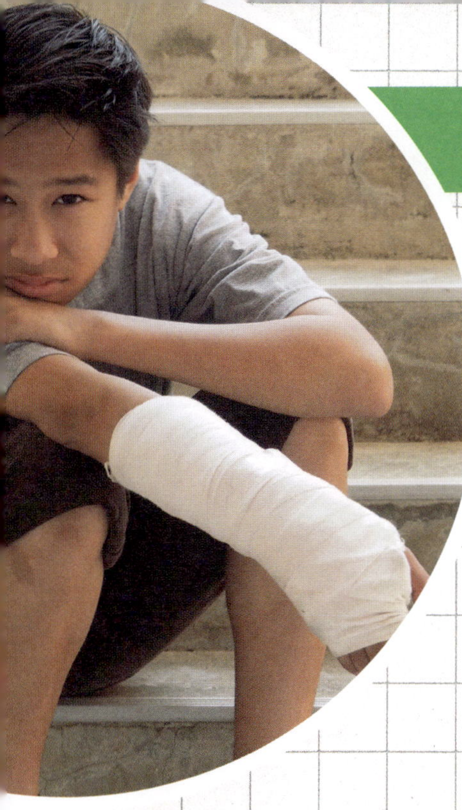

Whilst Job is "wearing sackcloth and ashes", three of his friends come to visit. They wonder why Job has to suffer so much. In the end, God himself answers that question. He looks at things as the creator God. He knows and sees so much more than Job and his friends.

Read some verses from Job 38, 39, and 40.

"Where were you when I laid the earth's foundation? Tell me, if you understand. Who marked off its dimensions? Surely you know! Who stretched a measuring line across it?"
Job 38:4–5

A VERY SMALL PART

You need: camera, laptop or PC

Take a picture of each other, then upload it to a computer and open it. Zoom in as much as possible. What can you see? Are you still recognizable? Do you still like the photos?

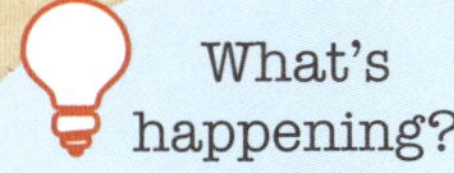

What's happening?

When you enlarge a photo, you will see small squares: "pixels". Each digital picture is made up of thousands of pixels, each with their own colour. Together they make the complete picture.

God sees the complete picture: what is, what was, and what is still to happen. We only see a tiny bit.

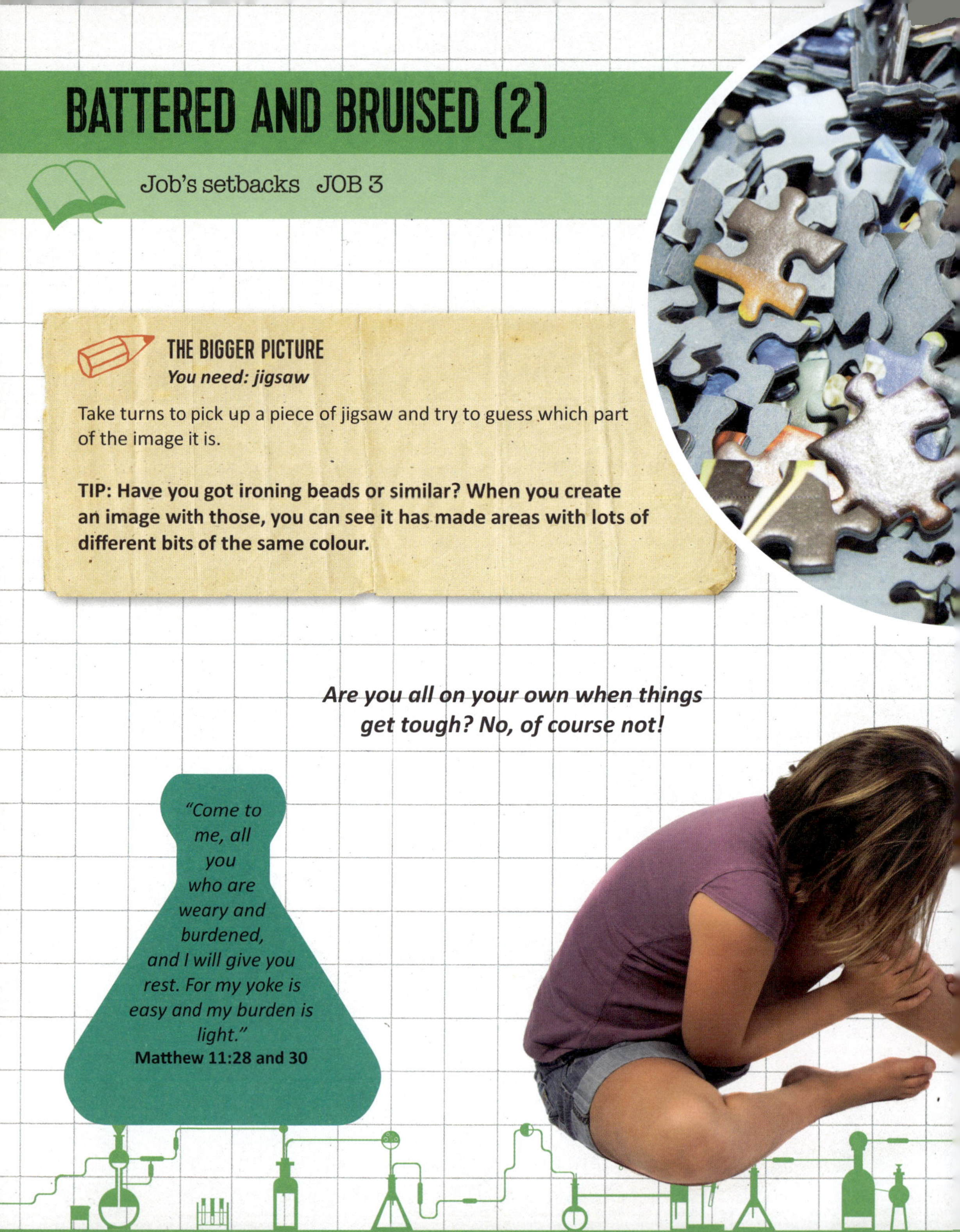

BATTERED AND BRUISED (2)

Job's setbacks JOB 3

THE BIGGER PICTURE

You need: jigsaw

Take turns to pick up a piece of jigsaw and try to guess which part of the image it is.

TIP: Have you got ironing beads or similar? When you create an image with those, you can see it has made areas with lots of different bits of the same colour.

Are you all on your own when things get tough? No, of course not!

"Come to me, all you who are weary and burdened, and I will give you rest. For my yoke is easy and my burden is light."
Matthew 11:28 and 30

YOU ARE NOT ALONE

You need: marble (adults should use a big marble)

Cross your index and your middle finger. Roll the marble underneath your crossed fingers front to back. It feels like two marbles!

Do you want to know how things end for Job? Read Job 41:10–17.

WHEN IS SOMETHING...

Air and emptiness ECCLESIASTES 1

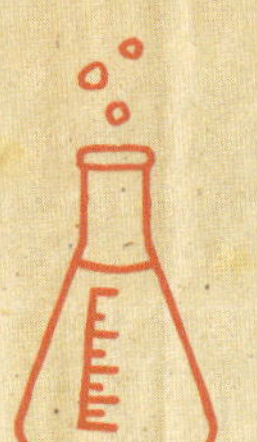

WHEN THERE'S NO MORE AIR...

You need: empty wine bottle (ideally see-through), wine bottle vacuum stopper (a stopper that doubles up as a vacuum pump), bucket with water

The wine bottle looks empty, but it's full of air. Push the bottle upside down into the water. What's happening? Put the vacuum stopper on the empty bottle and pump until all the air has come out. Now the bottle is truly empty.
Push the empty (and sealed) bottle upside down into the water. Remove the stopper. What happens next?

"Meaningless!
Meaningless!"
says the Teacher.
"Utterly meaningless!
Everything is meaningless."
Ecclesiastes 1:2

What's happening?

The first time you pushed down the bottle into the bucket, the water couldn't enter the bottle because the bottle was filled with air. The air was blocking the water. The second time, the air had all been pumped out of the bottle and the bottle was truly empty. There was room for the water. Why do you think the water level in the bucket rose when some of the water filled the bottle? Air pushes against everything, including the water in the bucket. This is "air pressure". Inside the bottle there is hardly any or no air pressure because you've pumped the air out. The air pressure against the water in the bucket is stronger than the air pressure inside the bottle and pushes the water into the bottle.

REALLY EMPTY?

Airtight packaging is used to keep food fresh for longer.

I have seen all the things that are done under the sun; all of them are meaningless, a chasing after the wind.
Ecclesiastes 1:14

STRONG AIR

You need: old CD, scissors, lighter

The CD is made from a hard material. You can test this by tapping it with your finger. Did you know you can create bubbles with the CD? Place the CD on the table with the right side up. Scratch the CD with the scissors until some has become see-through. Use the lighter to warm up the underside of the CD for about ten seconds and blow against this side. What can you see? If nothing happens, try to heat the same bit again and blow.

ASK AN ADULT TO HELP YOU.

What's happening?

The CD is made out of plastic. When you warm up the CD, it melts. The air you blow against and into the CD stretches the plastic and bubbles are formed.

A further thought:

You can't see air and you can't touch or grab it. But you have discovered the power of air in these two experiments.

FEAR

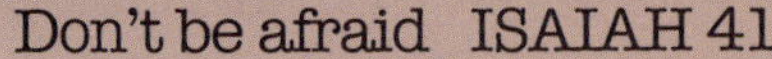

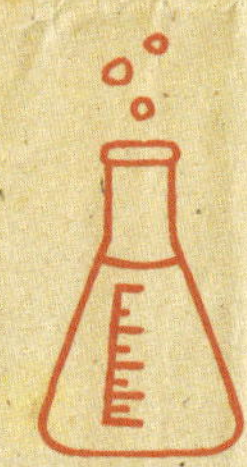

DO YOU DARE TO DO THIS?

You need: 3 balloons, needle, sticky tape, piece of orange peel (fresh)

Blow up and tie a balloon. Do you dare to pierce and pop it with a needle? Or are you afraid of the loud bang? Blow up and tie the second balloon. What happens when you squeeze orange peel against a balloon? The balloon pops, even if you don't touch it! Fear can make you angry or you may do things you don't really want to do. You can compare this fear with the orange peel.

Blow up and tie the third balloon and stick some sticky tape on the balloon in the shape of the cross. Pierce the balloon with the needle in the middle of the cross of tape.

So do not fear, for I am with you;
do not be dismayed, for I am your God.
I will strengthen you and help you.
Isaiah 41:10a

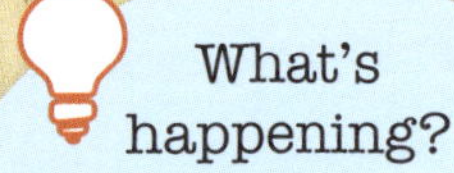

Orange peel contains a liquid, limonene, which comes out when you squeeze it. Balloons pop when limonene touches the rubber, which dissolves immediately.

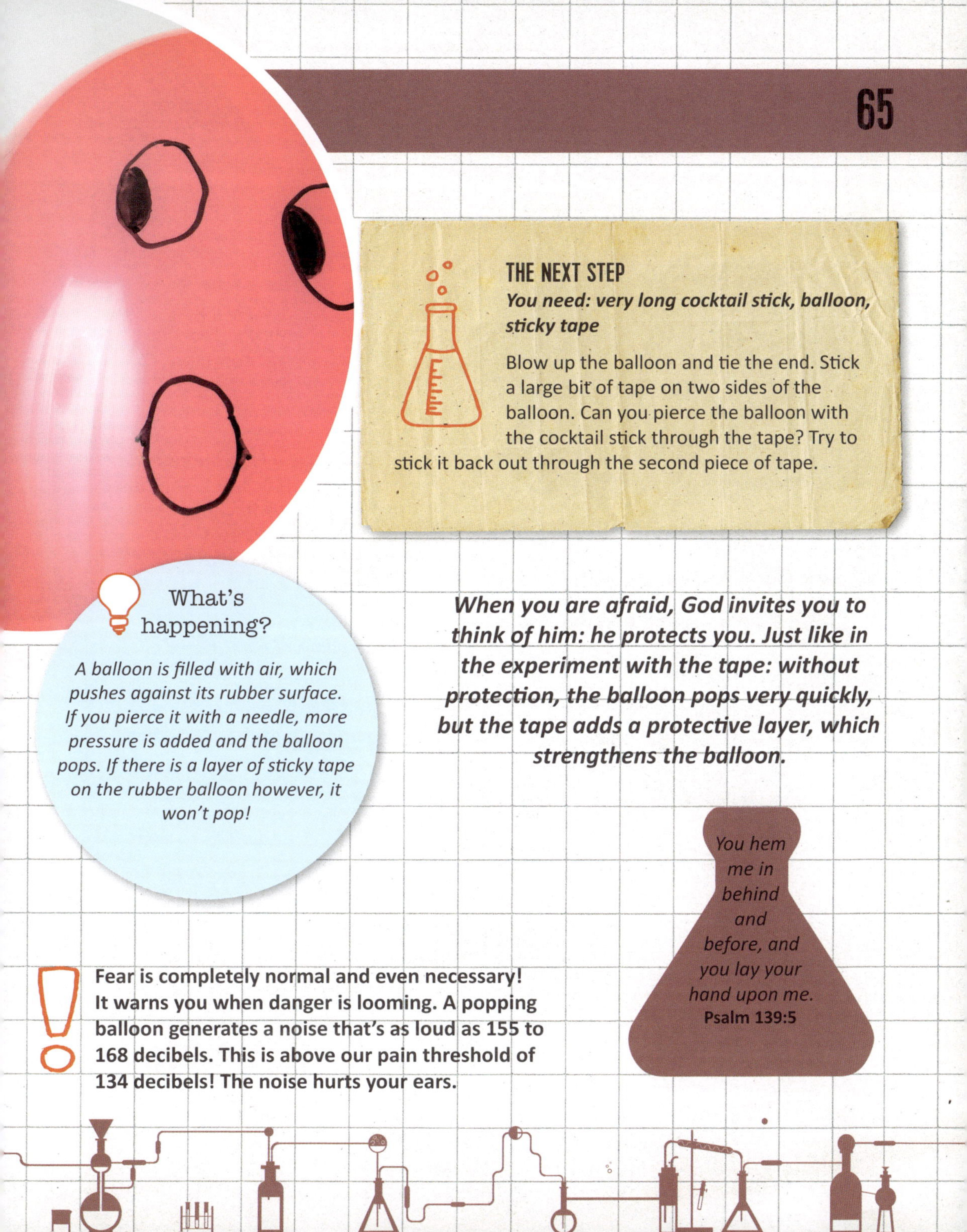

THE NEXT STEP

You need: very long cocktail stick, balloon, sticky tape

Blow up the balloon and tie the end. Stick a large bit of tape on two sides of the balloon. Can you pierce the balloon with the cocktail stick through the tape? Try to stick it back out through the second piece of tape.

What's happening?

A balloon is filled with air, which pushes against its rubber surface. If you pierce it with a needle, more pressure is added and the balloon pops. If there is a layer of sticky tape on the rubber balloon however, it won't pop!

When you are afraid, God invites you to think of him: he protects you. Just like in the experiment with the tape: without protection, the balloon pops very quickly, but the tape adds a protective layer, which strengthens the balloon.

You hem me in behind and before, and you lay your hand upon me.
Psalm 139:5

Fear is completely normal and even necessary! It warns you when danger is looming. A popping balloon generates a noise that's as loud as 155 to 168 decibels. This is above our pain threshold of 134 decibels! The noise hurts your ears.

LIKE CLAY IN THE HANDS...

Jeremiah at the potter's JEREMIAH 18

"Go down to the potter's house, and there I will give you my message." So I went down to the potter's house, and I saw him working at the wheel. But the pot he was shaping from the clay was marred in his hands; so the potter formed it into another pot, shaping it as seemed best to him.
Jeremiah 18:2–4

A further thought:

Then the word of the Lord came to me. He said, "Can I not do with you, Israel, as this potter does?" declares the Lord. "Like clay in the hand of the potter, so are you in my hand, Israel."
Jeremiah 18:5–6

MAKE YOUR OWN CLAY

You need: 2 cups of flour, 2 cups of salt, wooden spoon, cup of water, 2 tablespoons of plant-based oil, bowl, food colouring

Put the flour and salt in the bowl and mix. Add the oil and then the water. Mix everything well and knead until any lumps have gone. Your clay is ready!

Tip: Split the clay several times and add different food colourings to each portion.

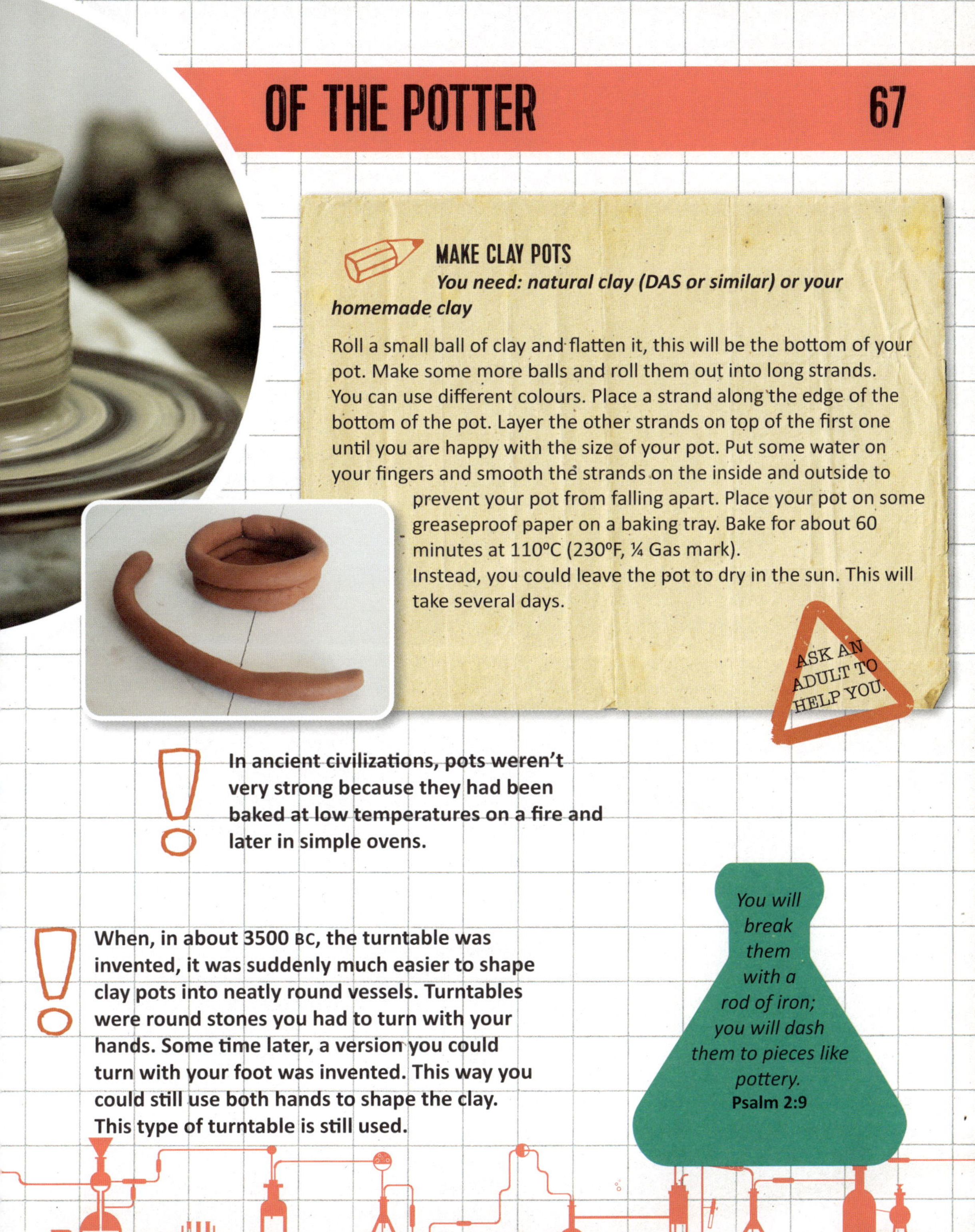

MAKE CLAY POTS

You need: natural clay (DAS or similar) or your homemade clay

Roll a small ball of clay and flatten it, this will be the bottom of your pot. Make some more balls and roll them out into long strands. You can use different colours. Place a strand along the edge of the bottom of the pot. Layer the other strands on top of the first one until you are happy with the size of your pot. Put some water on your fingers and smooth the strands on the inside and outside to prevent your pot from falling apart. Place your pot on some greaseproof paper on a baking tray. Bake for about 60 minutes at 110ºC (230ºF, ¼ Gas mark).
Instead, you could leave the pot to dry in the sun. This will take several days.

In ancient civilizations, pots weren't very strong because they had been baked at low temperatures on a fire and later in simple ovens.

When, in about 3500 BC, the turntable was invented, it was suddenly much easier to shape clay pots into neatly round vessels. Turntables were round stones you had to turn with your hands. Some time later, a version you could turn with your foot was invented. This way you could still use both hands to shape the clay. This type of turntable is still used.

You will break them with a rod of iron; you will dash them to pieces like pottery.
Psalm 2:9

A BEAUTIFUL FUTURE

God's words for Ezekiel EZEKIEL 34

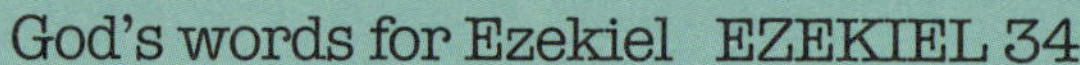

WHO WAS EZEKIEL?

God spoke these words to the prophet Ezekiel. Ezekiel lived in exile in Babylonia. He probably was a priest. Ezekiel shared the words about a beautiful future with other Jews who, just like him, had been forced to leave their country.

I will make them and the places surrounding my hill a blessing. I will send down showers in season; there will be showers of blessing. The trees will yield their fruit and the ground will yield its crops; the people will be secure in their land. They will know that I am the Lord, when I break the bars of their yoke and rescue them from the hands of those who enslaved them.
Ezekiel 34:26 and 27

LIKE FERTILE RAIN

You need: oil, water, large glass, small dish, green food colouring (supermarket)

Pour a layer of oil into the dish and mix in a few drops of food colouring. Fill the glass three quarters full with water. Pour the oil mixture into the water and leave it to settle. After a while you can see that more and more green drops will fall down to the bottom of the glass.

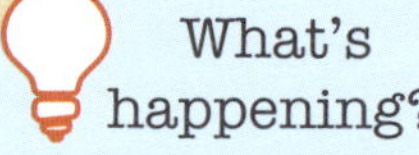

What's happening?

Oil and water are made up of molecules, very small particles. Water molecules pull at each other with such great force that they push the oil molecules away. Because of this, water and oil don't mix; they repel one another. The oil moves up as it's lighter than water.

The words of God filled the prophet Ezekiel and the Jewish people in exile with new hope.

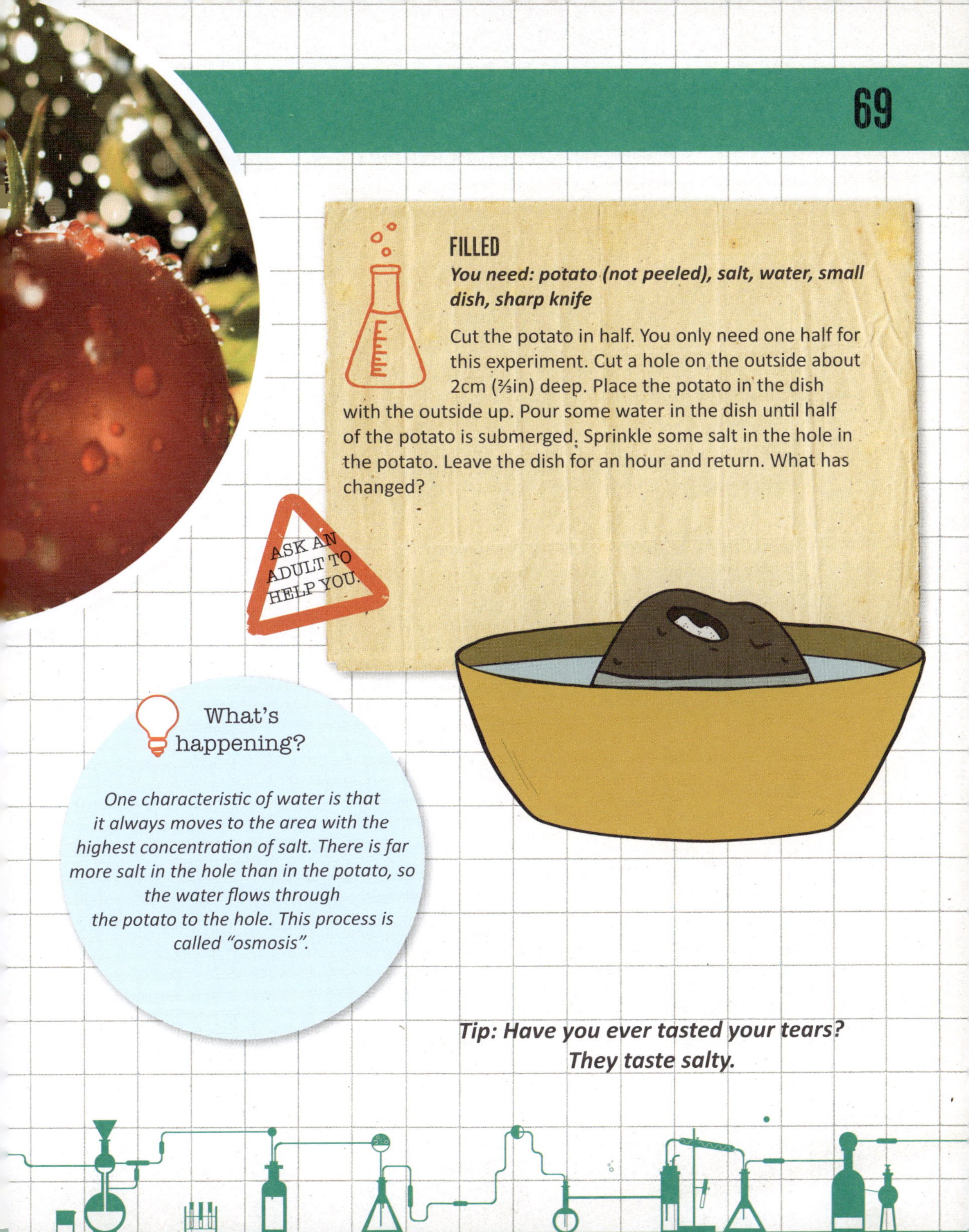

FILLED

You need: potato (not peeled), salt, water, small dish, sharp knife

Cut the potato in half. You only need one half for this experiment. Cut a hole on the outside about 2cm (⅔in) deep. Place the potato in the dish with the outside up. Pour some water in the dish until half of the potato is submerged. Sprinkle some salt in the hole in the potato. Leave the dish for an hour and return. What has changed?

What's happening?

One characteristic of water is that it always moves to the area with the highest concentration of salt. There is far more salt in the hole than in the potato, so the water flows through the potato to the hole. This process is called "osmosis".

Tip: Have you ever tasted your tears? They taste salty.

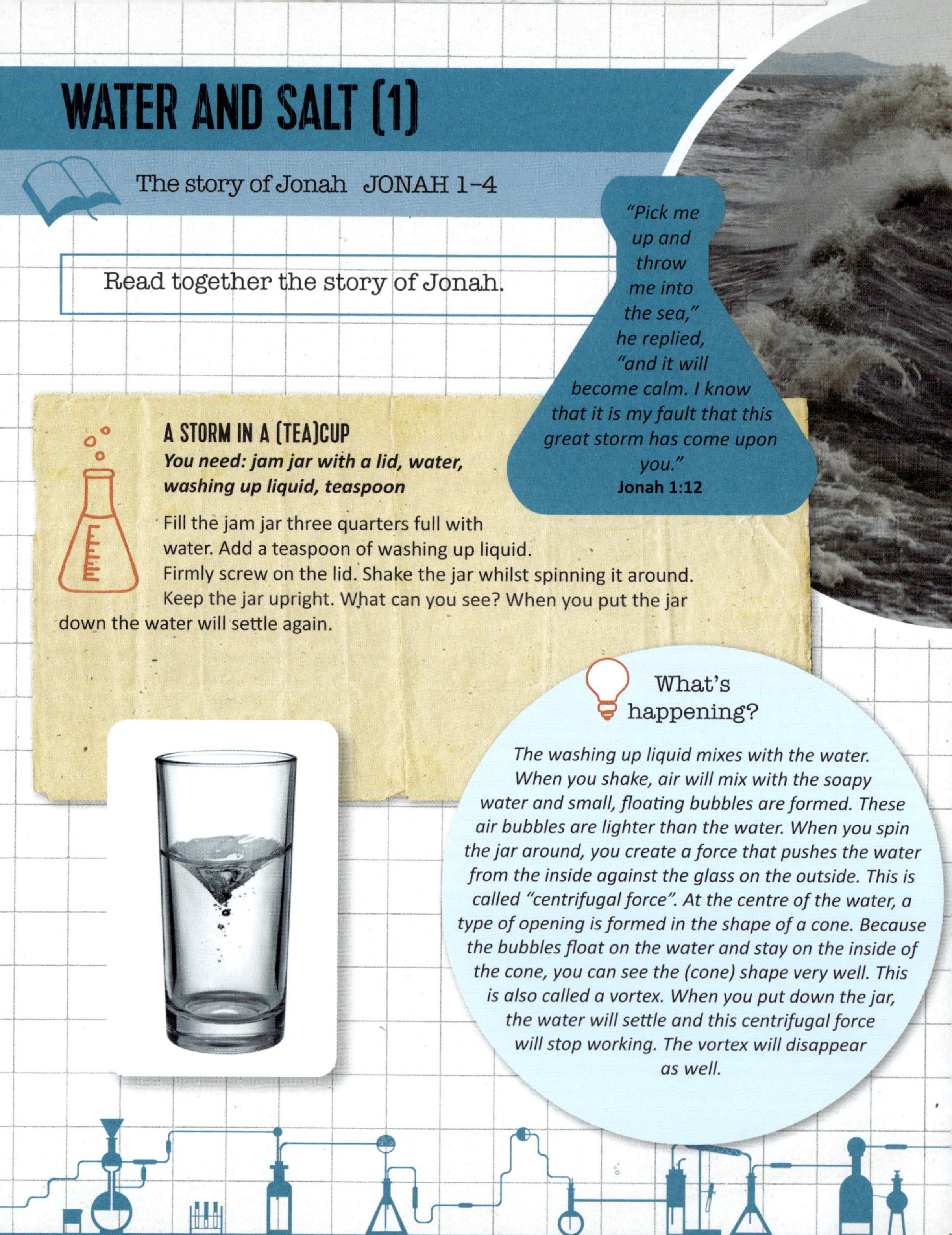

WATER AND SALT (1)

The story of Jonah JONAH 1–4

Read together the story of Jonah.

"Pick me up and throw me into the sea," he replied, "and it will become calm. I know that it is my fault that this great storm has come upon you."
Jonah 1:12

A STORM IN A (TEA)CUP

You need: jam jar with a lid, water, washing up liquid, teaspoon

Fill the jam jar three quarters full with water. Add a teaspoon of washing up liquid. Firmly screw on the lid. Shake the jar whilst spinning it around. Keep the jar upright. What can you see? When you put the jar down the water will settle again.

What's happening?

The washing up liquid mixes with the water. When you shake, air will mix with the soapy water and small, floating bubbles are formed. These air bubbles are lighter than the water. When you spin the jar around, you create a force that pushes the water from the inside against the glass on the outside. This is called "centrifugal force". At the centre of the water, a type of opening is formed in the shape of a cone. Because the bubbles float on the water and stay on the inside of the cone, you can see the (cone) shape very well. This is also called a vortex. When you put down the jar, the water will settle and this centrifugal force will stop working. The vortex will disappear as well.

CENTRIFUGAL FORCE AT HOME

You can also find centrifugal forces at work in your home. For instance a washing machine, when it spins at the end of a cycle. The drum, which has the laundry in, starts to spin very fast. Thanks to the "centrifugal force" the laundry is pushed against the walls of the drum. The force pushes the water out of the laundry.

Another example is a food blender. The small knives at the bottom turn around and create a centrifugal force. Make a fruit smoothie and see how the force of these knives pushes the fruit against the blender wall until it is crushed.

Then they took Jonah and threw him overboard, and the raging sea grew calm.
Jonah 1:15

WATER AND SALT (2)

The story of Jonah JONAH 1–4

Even though Jonah is extremely reluctant, he travels to Nineveh. He tells the people they must stop behaving badly or else God will destroy the city. Jonah is actually keen to see that happen. He finds a spot just outside the city to watch. But God doesn't do it! He saves Nineveh.

Why is Jonah so angry? Why isn't Jonah happy for the people of Nineveh?

You could say that Jonah is grumpy. He is filled with frustration, grumpiness, and negative thoughts. You can compare this with the salt in the water of the next experiment. The water is like positive and happy thoughts.

But to Jonah this seemed very wrong, and he became angry. He prayed to the Lord, "Isn't this what I said, Lord, when I was still at home? That is what I tried to avoid by fleeing to Tarshish. I knew that you are a gracious and compassionate God."
Jonah 4:1–2a

GRUMPY

You need: 2 glasses, water, salt, 2 fresh carrots, tablespoon

Fill both glasses with water. Add two tablespoons of salt to one of the glasses. Stir in the salt really well. Label this glass with a sticky note, so you remember it contains the salt. Place a carrot in each glass and leave it for the night before you check again. What has happened to the carrots?

What's happening?

The carrots contain water. The water keeps the carrot firm. Water always flows to the area with the highest salt concentration. Carrot cells only contain a small amount of salt, much less than in the glass with the salt solution. When you place the carrot in that glass, the water inside the carrot flows into the solution. The carrot loses all its water and becomes limp.

Read the end of the story in Jonah 4:4–11.

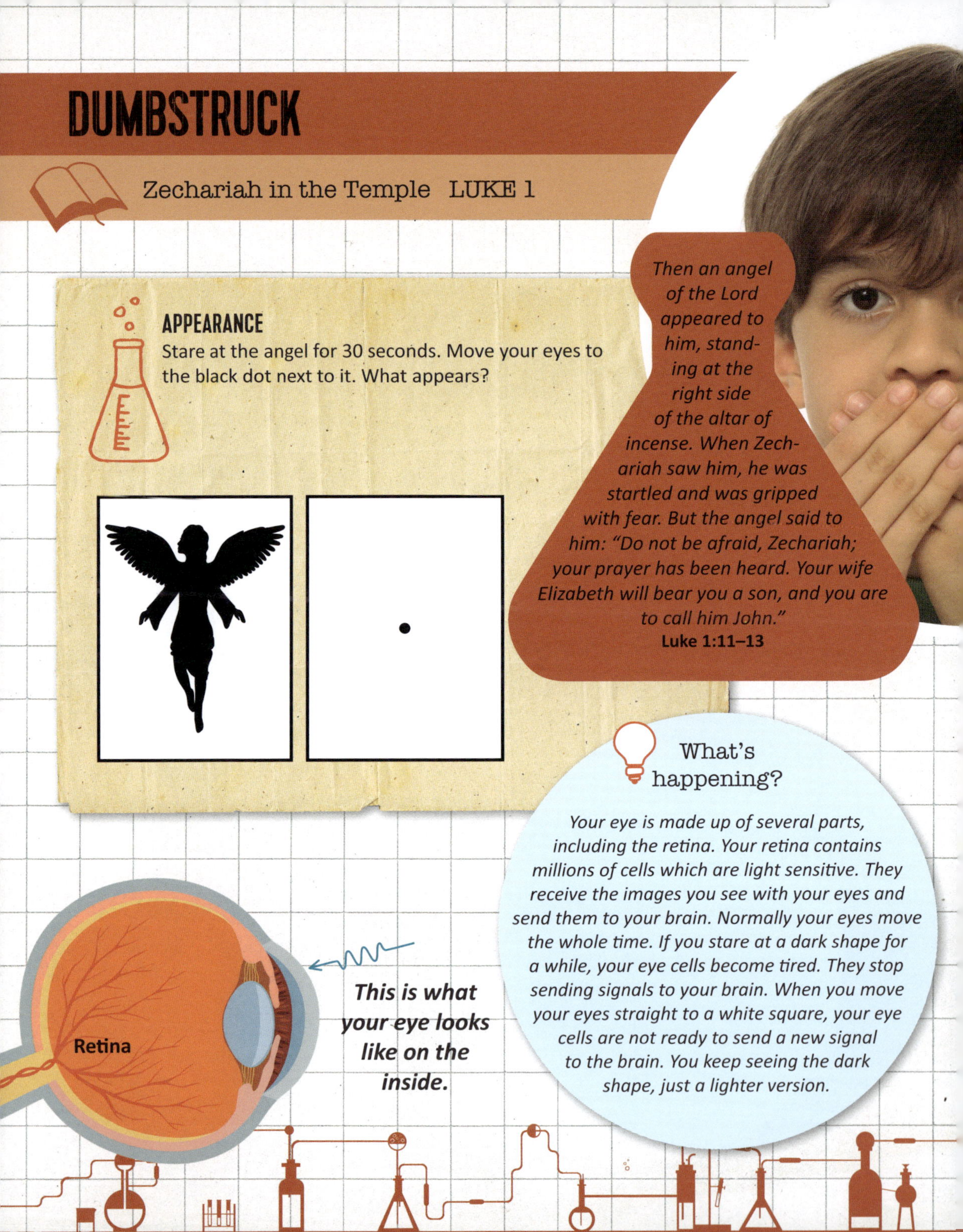

DUMBSTRUCK

Zechariah in the Temple LUKE 1

APPEARANCE

Stare at the angel for 30 seconds. Move your eyes to the black dot next to it. What appears?

Then an angel of the Lord appeared to him, standing at the right side of the altar of incense. When Zechariah saw him, he was startled and was gripped with fear. But the angel said to him: "Do not be afraid, Zechariah; your prayer has been heard. Your wife Elizabeth will bear you a son, and you are to call him John."

Luke 1:11–13

What's happening?

Your eye is made up of several parts, including the retina. Your retina contains millions of cells which are light sensitive. They receive the images you see with your eyes and send them to your brain. Normally your eyes move the whole time. If you stare at a dark shape for a while, your eye cells become tired. They stop sending signals to your brain. When you move your eyes straight to a white square, your eye cells are not ready to send a new signal to the brain. You keep seeing the dark shape, just a lighter version.

This is what your eye looks like on the inside.

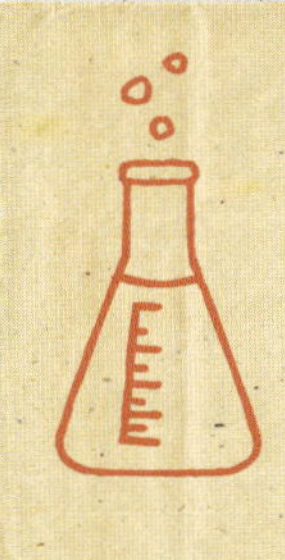

FEEL YOUR OWN SOUND WAVES

When you speak, you use your vocal chords. These vocal chords are inside your throat and you can feel them. Put your hand against your throat when you talk. What can you feel? What do you feel when you whisper?

The angel said to him, "I am Gabriel. I stand in the presence of God, and I have been sent to speak to you and to tell you this good news. And now you will be silent and not able to speak until the day this happens, because you did not believe my words."
Luke 1:19–20a

What wasn't working inside Zechariah when he couldn't speak?

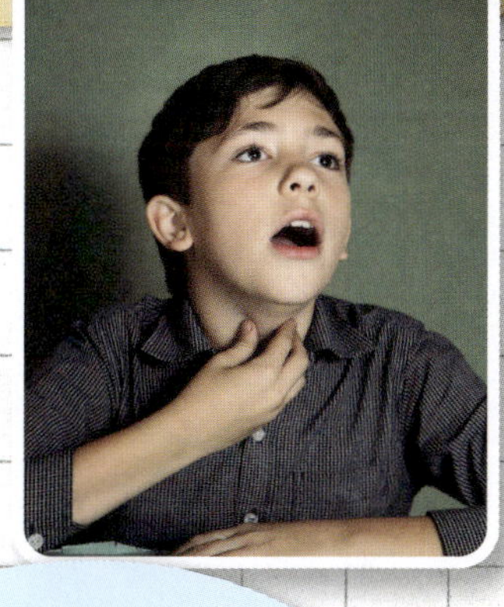

Bats can hear the highest frequencies. They transmit this high-pitched sound themselves. The sound waves hit their prey and they echo back to the bats, so they know where to catch their prey. In 2013 scientists discovered that the animal with the acutest sense of hearing is the greater wax moth. This moth is one of the main foods for bats. The moths' hearing developed to avoid getting caught by bats – an evolutionary response. Both species are constantly adapting to each other. This is called co-evolution.

What's happening?

Sound is created when something vibrates. The vibration sets the air in motion. These motions are called sound waves. When you speak, your vocal chords vibrate and sound waves are formed. You create these with your mouth, tongue, and lips. Your ears receive these sound waves as they "crash" against your eardrums, which start to vibrate. Small fibrils (hairs that vibrate) inside your ear send the signal on to your brain. Your brain transforms the signals into sound and matches this with knowledge inside the memory area of the brain, so that you will recognize the sound.

HOW MARY'S LIFE CHANGED

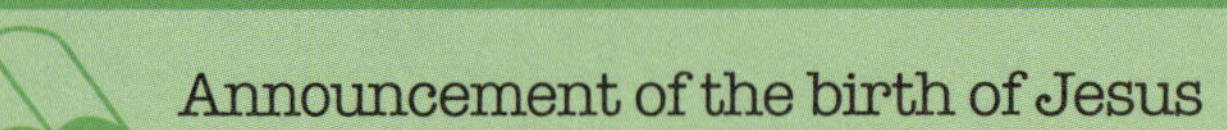

Announcement of the birth of Jesus LUKE 1

But the angel said to her, "Do not be afraid, Mary, you have found favour with God. You will conceive and give birth to a son, and you are to call him Jesus. He will be great and will be called the Son of the Most High."
Luke 1:30–32a

DYEING FLOWERS

You need: different colours of ink or liquid watercolour or food colouring, white flowers, small vases or glasses (or large test tubes), water

Fill a number of vases with water. Mix each one with a different colour of ink. Place one or more white flowers in each vase. Wait and watch the flowers throughout the day. What's happening?

Tip: Instead of white flowers you can use white chicory leaves.

The angel answered, "The Holy Spirit will come on you, and the power of the Most High will overshadow you."
Luke 1:35a

What's happening?

A flower drinks (absorbs) water through channels within its stem. The dye in the water is sucked up at the same time and absorbed by the flower. The water leaves the petals when it evaporates (turns to vapour), but the dye stays behind.

The Holy Spirit filled Mary just like the ink that filled and dyed the flowers. Just remember: this is only a comparison! The way the Holy Spirit filled Mary, so she could conceive the Lord Jesus is of course much more miraculous than this experiment.

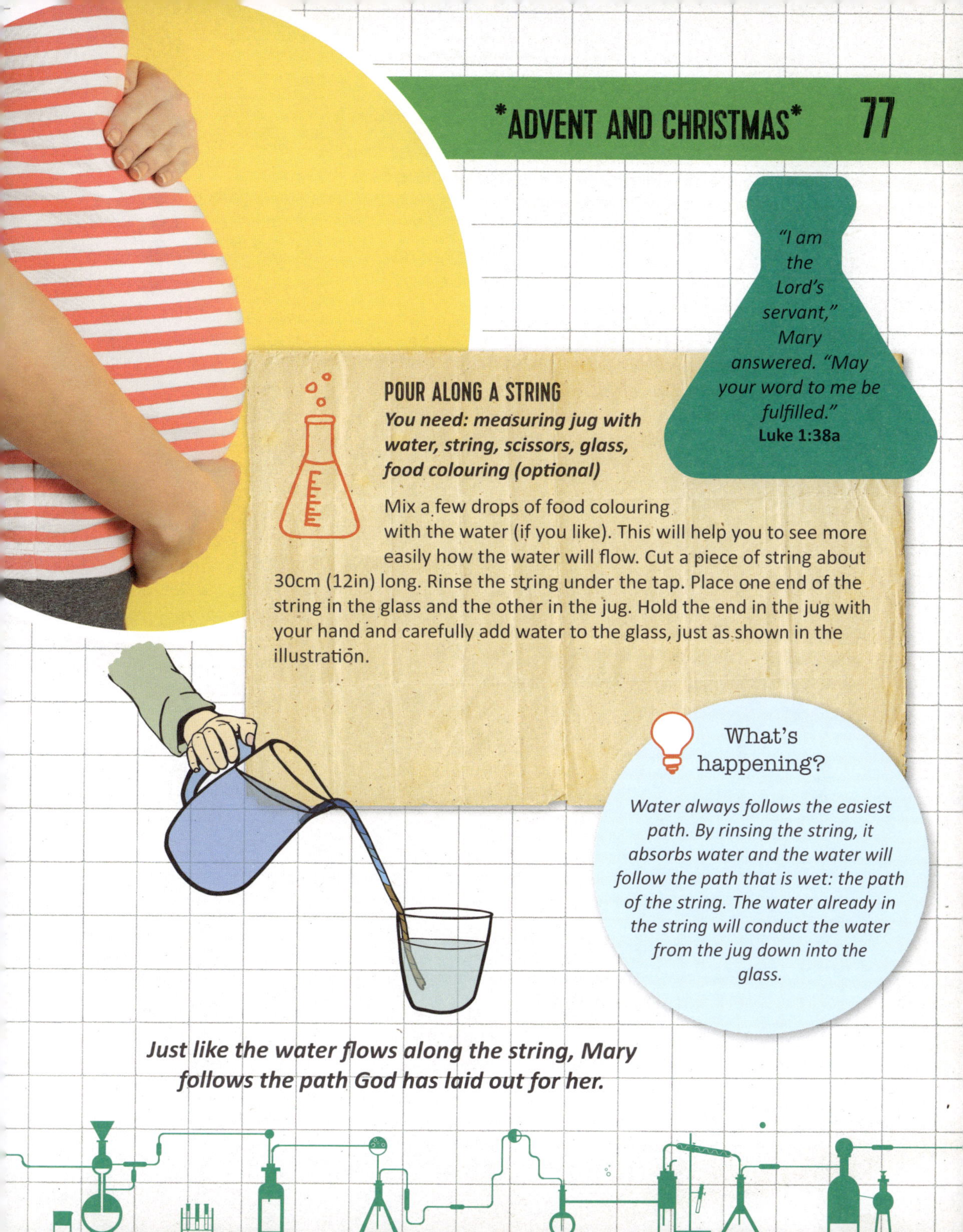

"I am the Lord's servant," Mary answered. "May your word to me be fulfilled."
Luke 1:38a

POUR ALONG A STRING

You need: measuring jug with water, string, scissors, glass, food colouring (optional)

Mix a few drops of food colouring with the water (if you like). This will help you to see more easily how the water will flow. Cut a piece of string about 30cm (12in) long. Rinse the string under the tap. Place one end of the string in the glass and the other in the jug. Hold the end in the jug with your hand and carefully add water to the glass, just as shown in the illustration.

What's happening?

Water always follows the easiest path. By rinsing the string, it absorbs water and the water will follow the path that is wet: the path of the string. The water already in the string will conduct the water from the jug down into the glass.

Just like the water flows along the string, Mary follows the path God has laid out for her.

DISSOLVED!

Joseph's dream MATTHEW 1

Joseph is worried; he's got a problem. Mary is pregnant, but not by him... How can he resolve this in the best way?

But after he had considered this, an angel of the Lord appeared to him in a dream and said, "Joseph son of David, do not be afraid to take Mary home as your wife, because what is conceived in her is from the Holy Spirit. She will give birth to a son, and you are to give him the name Jesus."
Matthew 1:20–21a

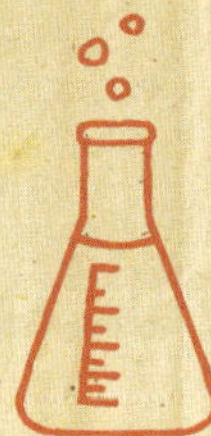

VANISHING MATERIAL

You need: nail varnish remover containing acetone, fairly small dish (glass or china), small pieces of material made of viscose (acetate-rayon), for instance an old tie or nightie.

Tip: Viscose (or rayon) is artificial silk, just check the label of the garment to make sure that it is made of the right material.

Pour a generous layer of nail varnish remover into the dish. Plunge the material into the dish. Wait for a bit and then take it out. What has happened to the material?

Cast all your anxiety on him because he cares for you.
1 Peter 5:7

What's happening?

Acetone breaks down the acetate-rayon into very small bits, loose molecules. These molecules don't dissolve but float around in the acetone. However, they are too small to see with the naked eye. It looks as if the material has completely vanished.

Sometimes you can't see what the best solution is, just as your eyes don't always see what they are supposed to be seeing.

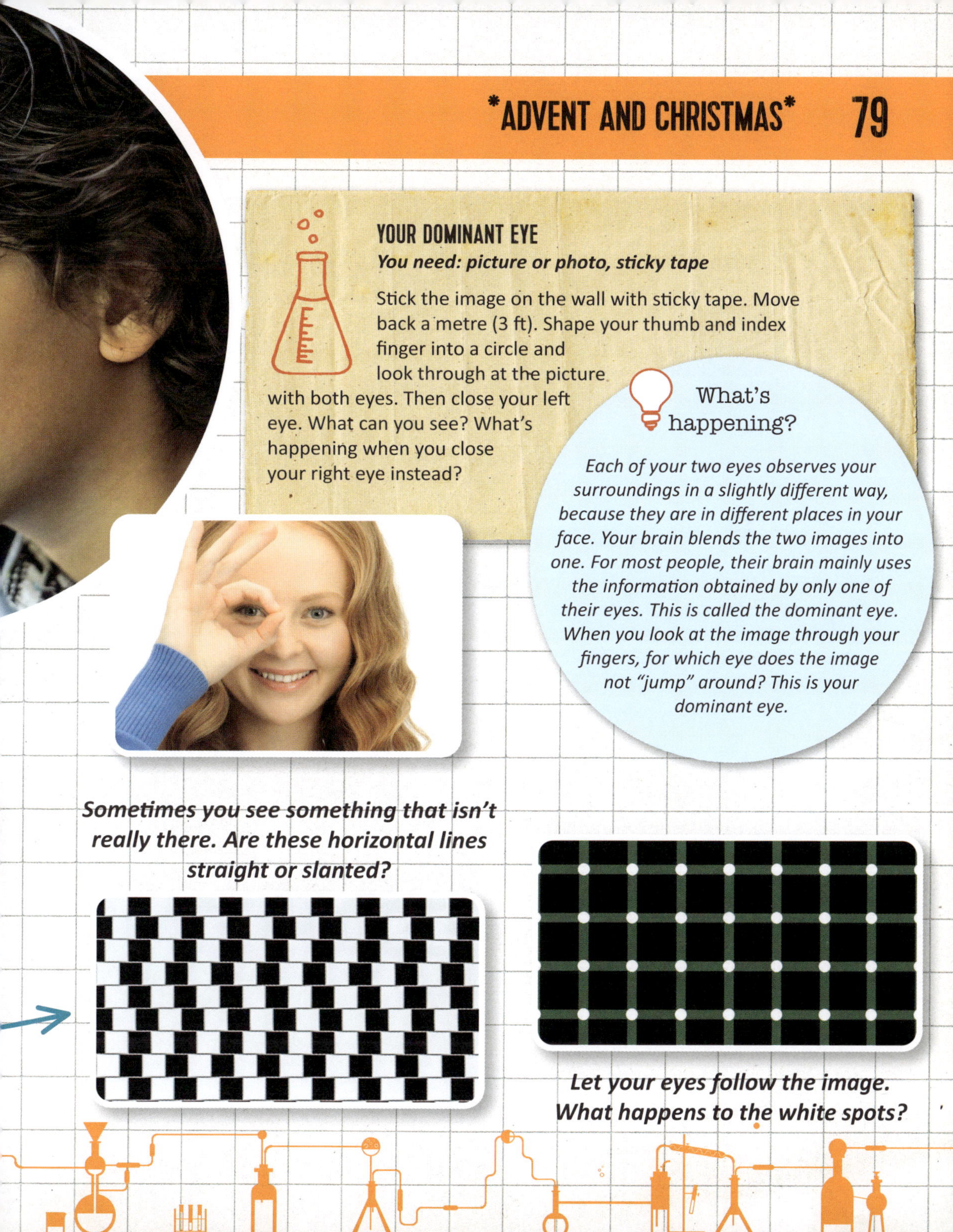

YOUR DOMINANT EYE

You need: picture or photo, sticky tape

Stick the image on the wall with sticky tape. Move back a metre (3 ft). Shape your thumb and index finger into a circle and look through at the picture with both eyes. Then close your left eye. What can you see? What's happening when you close your right eye instead?

What's happening?

Each of your two eyes observes your surroundings in a slightly different way, because they are in different places in your face. Your brain blends the two images into one. For most people, their brain mainly uses the information obtained by only one of their eyes. This is called the dominant eye. When you look at the image through your fingers, for which eye does the image not "jump" around? This is your dominant eye.

Sometimes you see something that isn't really there. Are these horizontal lines straight or slanted?

Let your eyes follow the image. What happens to the white spots?

FANTASTIC NEWS!

The Saviour has been born LUKE 2

But the angel said to them, "Do not be afraid. I bring you good news that will cause great joy for all the people. Today in the town of David a Saviour has been born to you; he is the Messiah, the Lord."
Luke 2:10–11

STRING PHONE

You need: two children, two empty tins, string about 3m (9ft) long, hammer and nail or awl

Make sure the tins are open at the top. Make a hole in the bottom by hammering a nail or an awl into each tin. Make a thick knot in one end of the string. Push the other end through the hole in one of the tins (the knot should be on the inside of the tin). Push the string through the second tin. Watch your fingers or ask an adult to help you. This time, start on the outside. Tie a knot in the string once it's through. Give one tin to someone else and hold on to the other tin yourself. Walk away until the string is taut. One person talks into their tin and the other holds their tin to their ear. Can you hear each other?

ASK AN ADULT TO HELP YOU.

What's happening?

Sound consists of vibrations. These vibrations are called sound waves. When you talk into the tin, the sound waves travel via the string all the way to the other tin.

What brilliant news would you like to tell someone else?

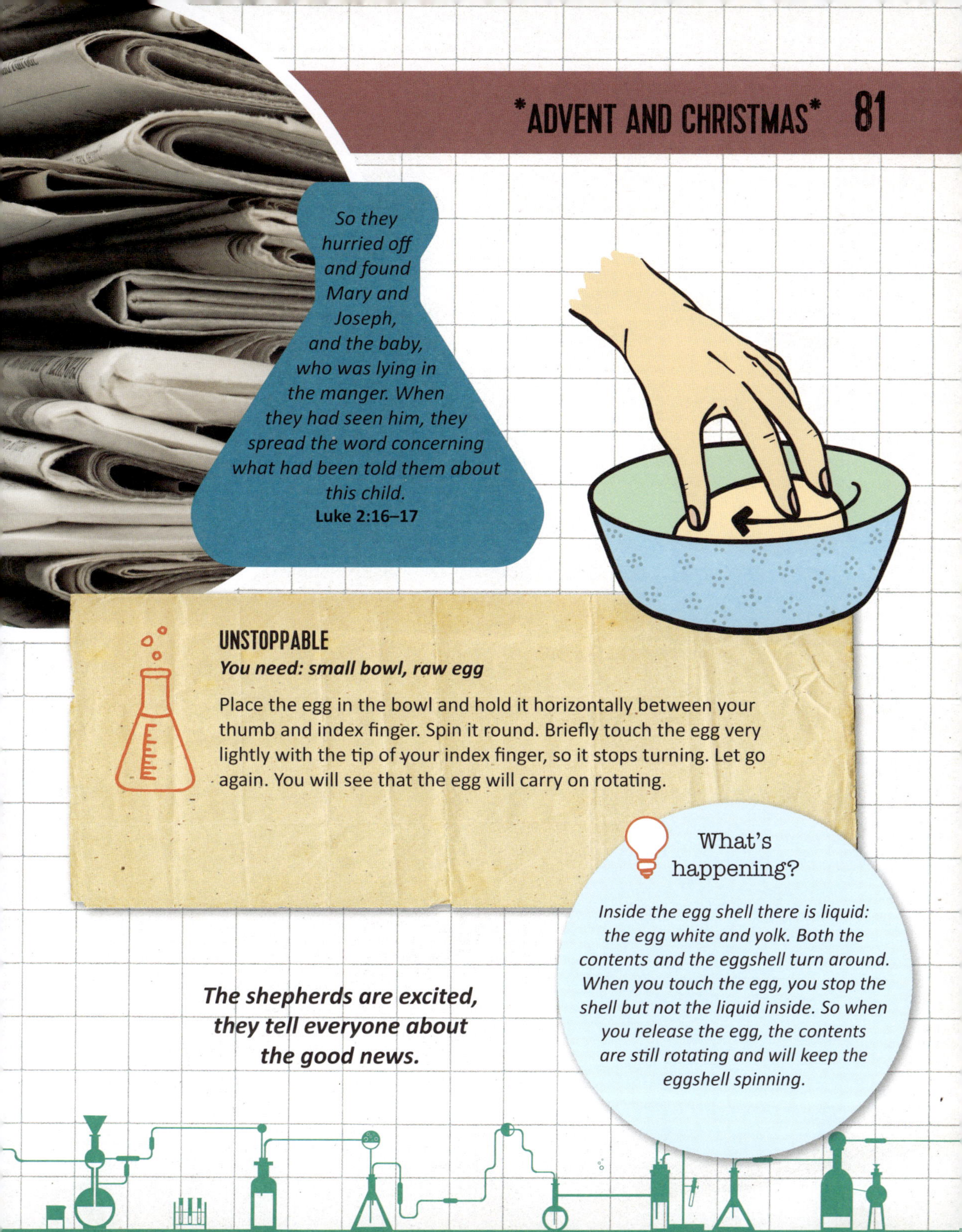

So they hurried off and found Mary and Joseph, and the baby, who was lying in the manger. When they had seen him, they spread the word concerning what had been told them about this child.
Luke 2:16–17

UNSTOPPABLE

You need: small bowl, raw egg

Place the egg in the bowl and hold it horizontally between your thumb and index finger. Spin it round. Briefly touch the egg very lightly with the tip of your index finger, so it stops turning. Let go again. You will see that the egg will carry on rotating.

What's happening?

Inside the egg shell there is liquid: the egg white and yolk. Both the contents and the eggshell turn around. When you touch the egg, you stop the shell but not the liquid inside. So when you release the egg, the contents are still rotating and will keep the eggshell spinning.

The shepherds are excited, they tell everyone about the good news.

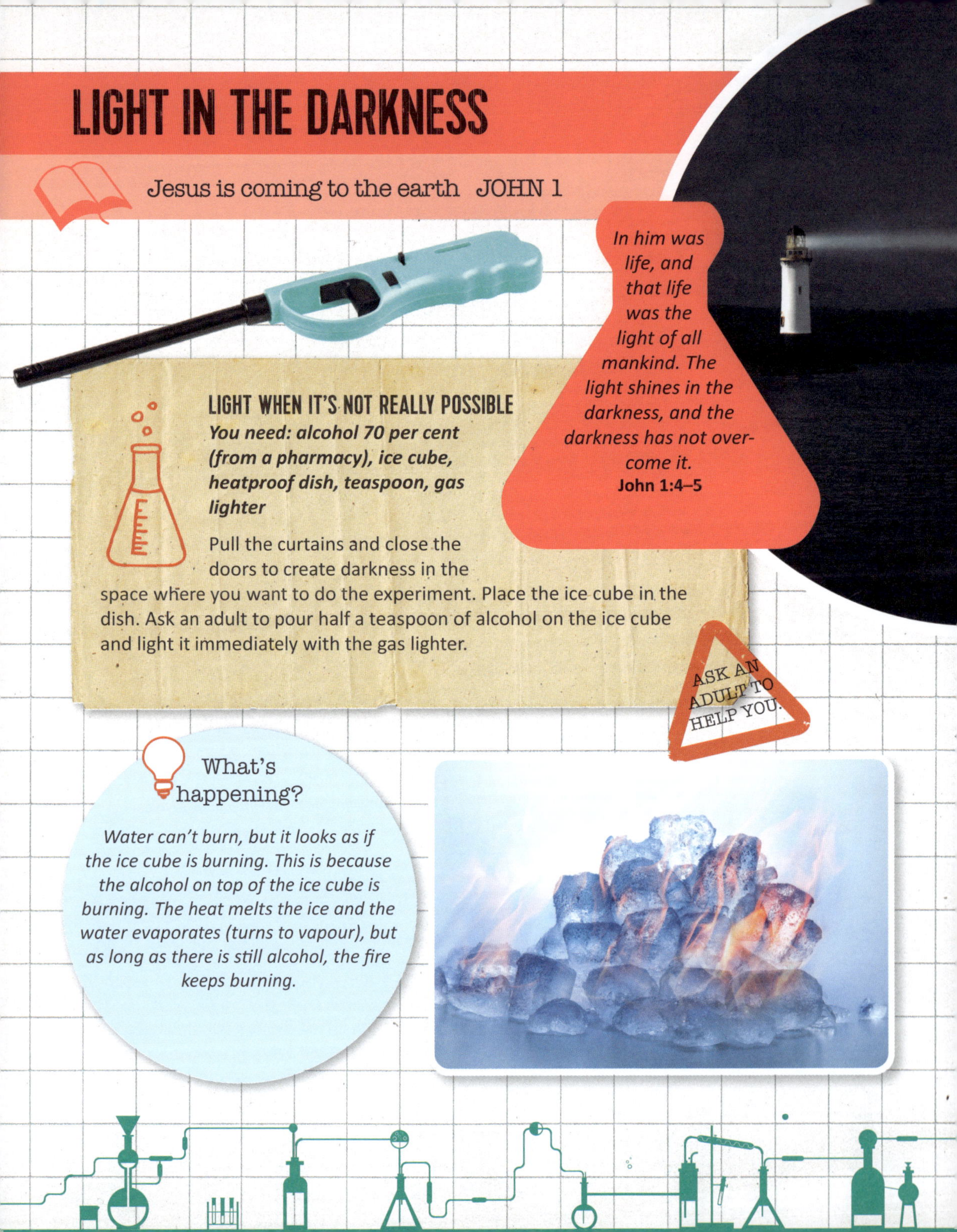

LIGHT IN THE DARKNESS

Jesus is coming to the earth JOHN 1

In him was life, and that life was the light of all mankind. The light shines in the darkness, and the darkness has not overcome it.
John 1:4–5

LIGHT WHEN IT'S NOT REALLY POSSIBLE

You need: alcohol 70 per cent (from a pharmacy), ice cube, heatproof dish, teaspoon, gas lighter

Pull the curtains and close the doors to create darkness in the space where you want to do the experiment. Place the ice cube in the dish. Ask an adult to pour half a teaspoon of alcohol on the ice cube and light it immediately with the gas lighter.

ASK AN ADULT TO HELP YOU.

What's happening?

Water can't burn, but it looks as if the ice cube is burning. This is because the alcohol on top of the ice cube is burning. The heat melts the ice and the water evaporates (turns to vapour), but as long as there is still alcohol, the fire keeps burning.

LITTLE FLAMES

You need: 15 tea lights, matches or gas lighter

Place the tea lights in a circle about 30cm (12in) across. Make sure that the tea lights are spaced out evenly. Ask an adult to light the tea lights. Wait a little (don't move) and watch the little flames. What do they look like at the start and how do they change?

What's happening?

The small flames warm up the air above the tea lights. Warm air rises. There is less air between the tea lights and the air pressure (see page 53) goes down. The air outside of the circle wants to move to the area with the lowest air pressure and it flows to the centre of the circle. This airflow moves the flames towards the centre too.

Read John 1:1–18 together and choose a few verses to create a work of art.

WAITING PATIENTLY

Simeon in the Temple LUKE 2

It had been revealed to him by the Holy Spirit that he would not die before he had seen the Lord's Messiah. Moved by the Spirit, he went into the Temple courts. When the parents brought in the child Jesus to do for him what the custom of the Law required, Simeon took him in his arms and praised God, saying: "Sovereign Lord, as you have promised, you may now dismiss your servant in peace."

Luke 2:26–29

GROWING IN PATIENCE

You need: 250ml (8½fl oz) water, 600g (21oz) of granulated sugar, tall slim glass, cocktail stick, peg, small clean paintbrush, food colouring, small pan, wooden spoon

Add the water and sugar to the pan. Ask an adult to help you heat it up on the hob. Stir until all the sugar has dissolved. Add about ten drops of food colouring and stir. Leave the mixture to cool.

Clip the peg onto the end of the cocktail stick. Use the brush to "paint" the stick with the mixture. Leave to dry thoroughly. Pour the cooled down mixture from the pan into the glass. Rest the peg on the rim with the cocktail stick in the mixture. Make sure the cocktail stick doesn't touch the bottom or glass.

Put the glass carefully in a dark, quiet spot and wait patiently. Remove the cocktail stick after 7–10 days and leave to dry. What do you see?

Tip: You can eat the sugar crystals!

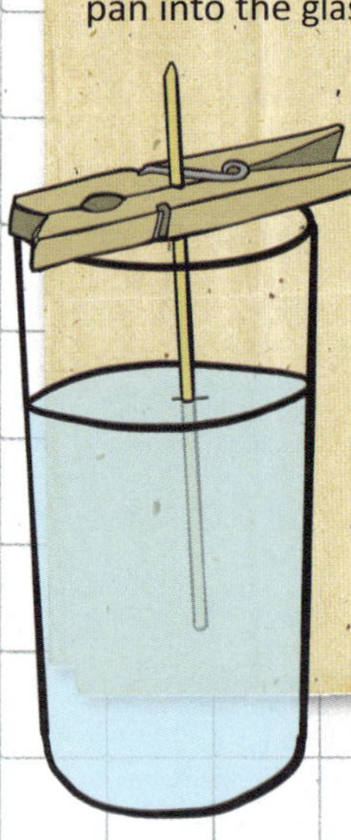

What's happening?

Sugar is made up of tiny particles: sugar molecules. The sugar has been mixed in with the water, but the sugar molecules keep attracting each other and stick together. They form sparkling crystals.

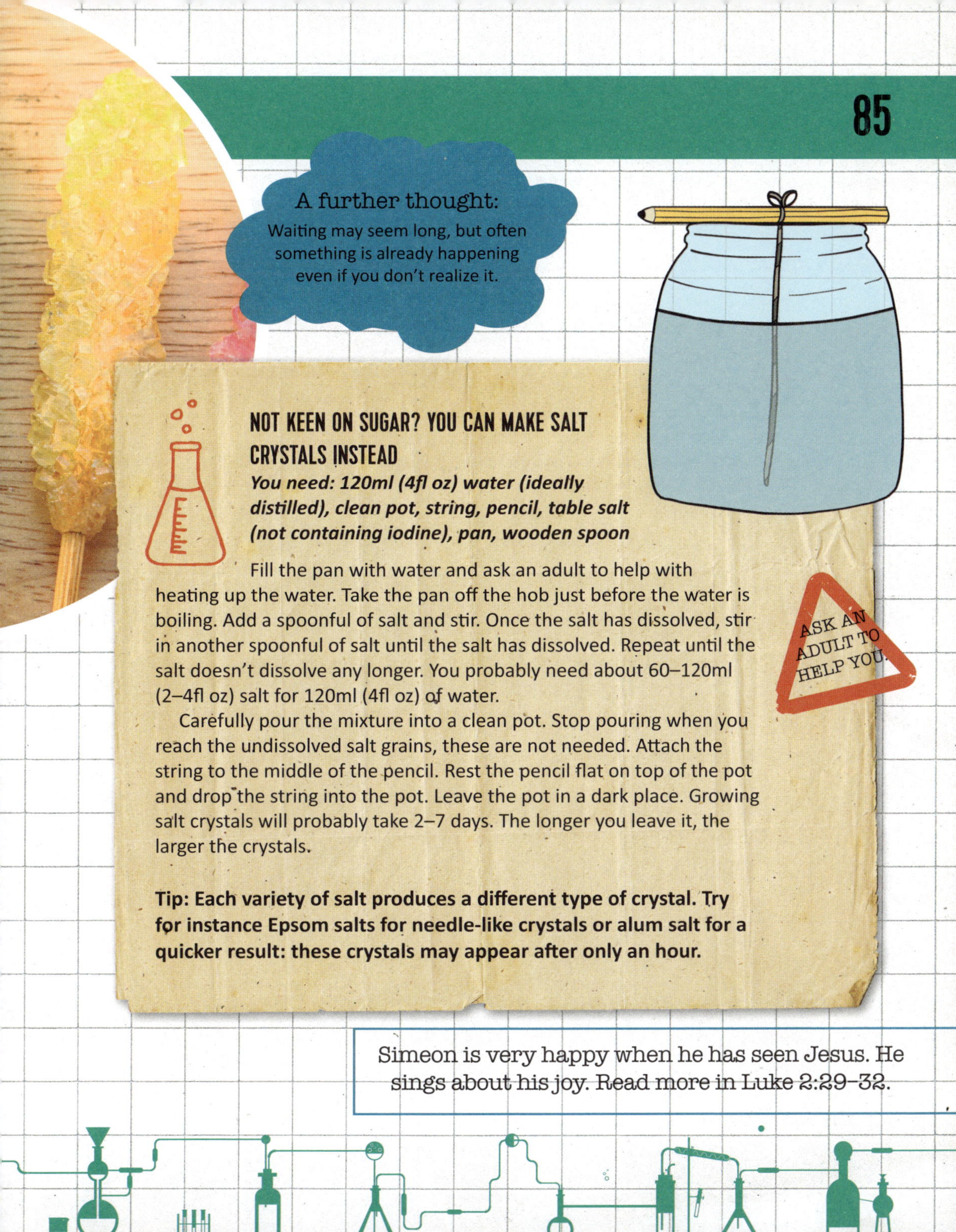

A further thought:

Waiting may seem long, but often something is already happening even if you don't realize it.

NOT KEEN ON SUGAR? YOU CAN MAKE SALT CRYSTALS INSTEAD

You need: 120ml (4fl oz) water (ideally distilled), clean pot, string, pencil, table salt (not containing iodine), pan, wooden spoon

Fill the pan with water and ask an adult to help with heating up the water. Take the pan off the hob just before the water is boiling. Add a spoonful of salt and stir. Once the salt has dissolved, stir in another spoonful of salt until the salt has dissolved. Repeat until the salt doesn't dissolve any longer. You probably need about 60–120ml (2–4fl oz) salt for 120ml (4fl oz) of water.

Carefully pour the mixture into a clean pot. Stop pouring when you reach the undissolved salt grains, these are not needed. Attach the string to the middle of the pencil. Rest the pencil flat on top of the pot and drop the string into the pot. Leave the pot in a dark place. Growing salt crystals will probably take 2–7 days. The longer you leave it, the larger the crystals.

Tip: Each variety of salt produces a different type of crystal. Try for instance Epsom salts for needle-like crystals or alum salt for a quicker result: these crystals may appear after only an hour.

Simeon is very happy when he has seen Jesus. He sings about his joy. Read more in Luke 2:29–32.

ASTRONOMY

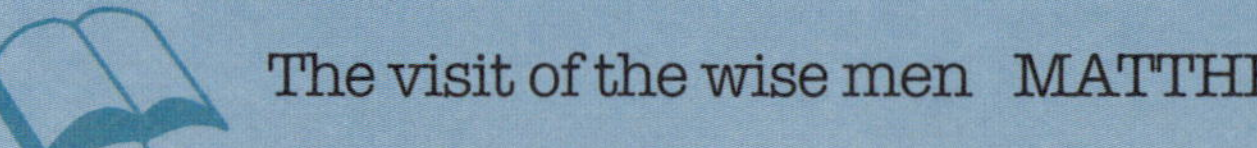

The visit of the wise men MATTHEW 2

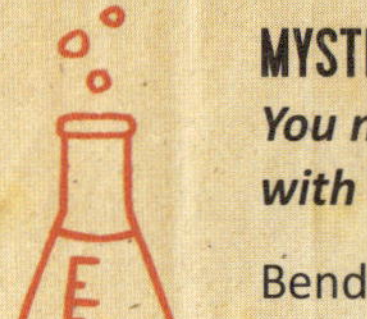

MYSTERIOUS STAR

You need: 5 wooden cocktail sticks, water, small bottle with dropper or pipette or small straw

Bend the five cocktail sticks in the middle. Make sure they don't completely snap. Make them into a star shape (see photograph). Make sure the ends of the sticks touch and that there is a small round shape in the middle. Use the bottle, pipette, or straw to put some drops of water in this circle. The sticks will move and form a new star shape!

...and they asked, "Where is the one who has been born king of the Jews? We saw his star when it rose and have come to worship him."
Matthew 2:2

What's happening?

The water pulls at the cocktail sticks where they are broken and then at the tips of the sticks. The sticks start to slide and move into a straighter position. In a way, the water flows into the sticks.

In the Middle Ages a quadrant was used to measure the distance between the horizon and a star or planet.

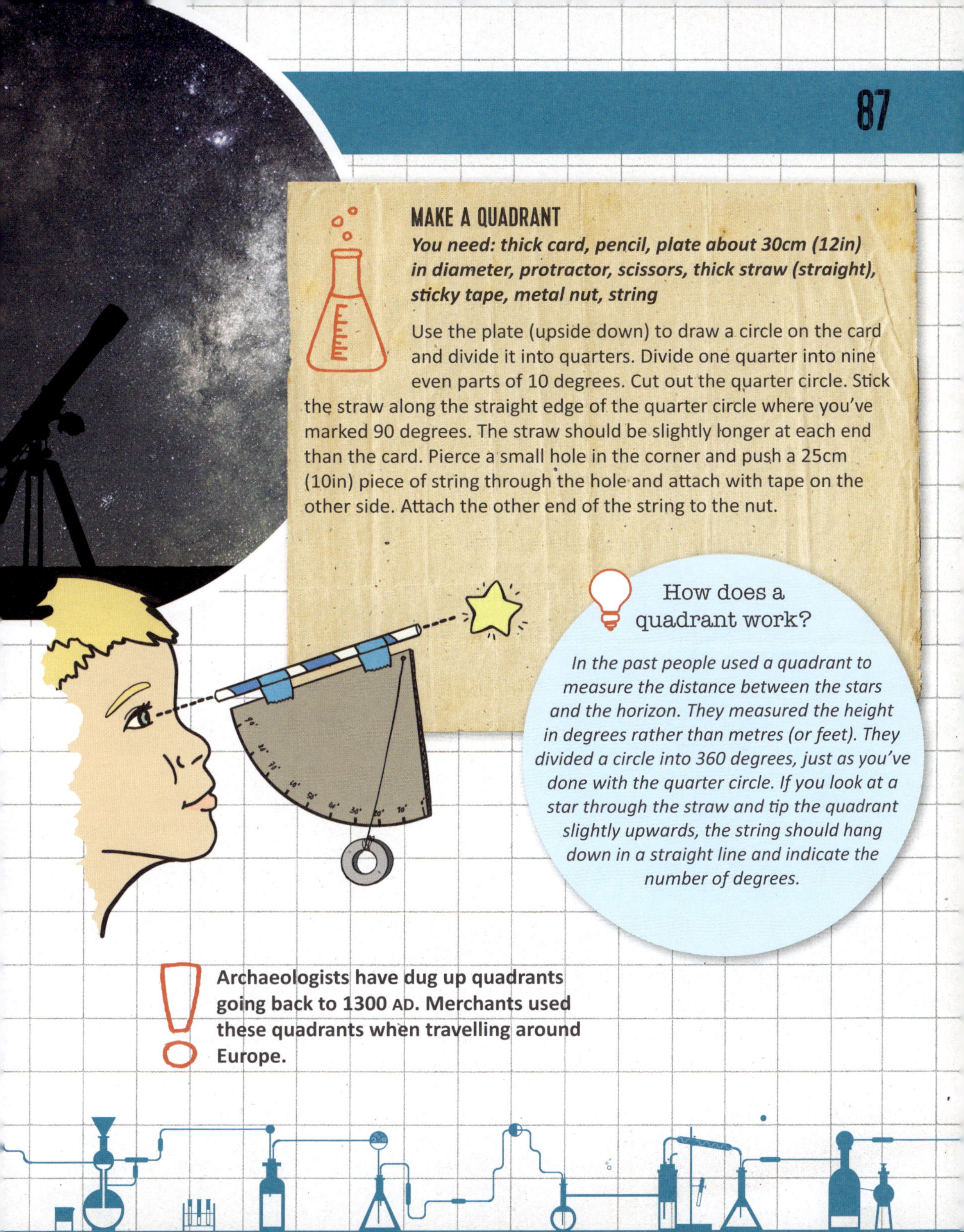

MAKE A QUADRANT

You need: thick card, pencil, plate about 30cm (12in) in diameter, protractor, scissors, thick straw (straight), sticky tape, metal nut, string

Use the plate (upside down) to draw a circle on the card and divide it into quarters. Divide one quarter into nine even parts of 10 degrees. Cut out the quarter circle. Stick the straw along the straight edge of the quarter circle where you've marked 90 degrees. The straw should be slightly longer at each end than the card. Pierce a small hole in the corner and push a 25cm (10in) piece of string through the hole and attach with tape on the other side. Attach the other end of the string to the nut.

How does a quadrant work?

In the past people used a quadrant to measure the distance between the stars and the horizon. They measured the height in degrees rather than metres (or feet). They divided a circle into 360 degrees, just as you've done with the quarter circle. If you look at a star through the straw and tip the quadrant slightly upwards, the string should hang down in a straight line and indicate the number of degrees.

Archaeologists have dug up quadrants going back to 1300 AD. Merchants used these quadrants when travelling around Europe.

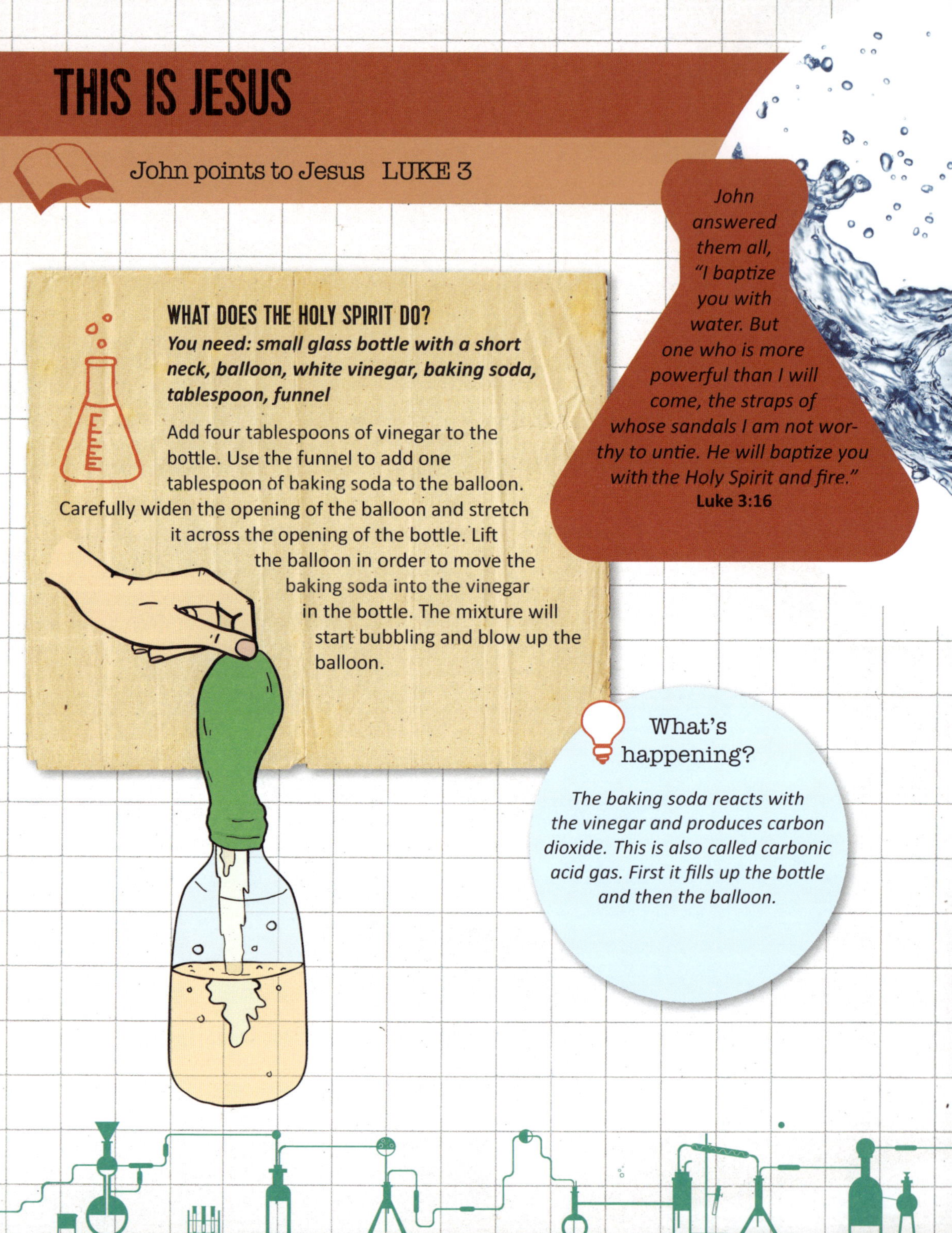

THIS IS JESUS

John points to Jesus LUKE 3

John answered them all, "I baptize you with water. But one who is more powerful than I will come, the straps of whose sandals I am not worthy to untie. He will baptize you with the Holy Spirit and fire."
Luke 3:16

WHAT DOES THE HOLY SPIRIT DO?

You need: small glass bottle with a short neck, balloon, white vinegar, baking soda, tablespoon, funnel

Add four tablespoons of vinegar to the bottle. Use the funnel to add one tablespoon of baking soda to the balloon. Carefully widen the opening of the balloon and stretch it across the opening of the bottle. Lift the balloon in order to move the baking soda into the vinegar in the bottle. The mixture will start bubbling and blow up the balloon.

What's happening?

The baking soda reacts with the vinegar and produces carbon dioxide. This is also called carbonic acid gas. First it fills up the bottle and then the balloon.

The Holy Spirit works just like the baking soda. He moves you and fills you.

When all the people were being baptized, Jesus was baptized too. And as he was praying, heaven was opened and the Holy Spirit descended on him in bodily form like a dove. And a voice came from heaven: "You are my Son, whom I love; with you I am well pleased."
Luke 3:21–22

WORDS THAT IMPRESS

Jesus teaches in the synagogue MARK 1

People sometimes say: "Those words have a powerful impact, they really hit home."

They went to Capernaum, and when the Sabbath came, Jesus went into the synagogue and began to teach. The people were amazed at his teaching.
Mark 1:21–22a

MAKE A CRATER AND MEASURE THE IMPACT OF THE MISSILE

You need: bowl or bucket, sand, tape measure, pen and paper, different types and sizes of marbles or other small balls (e.g. a golf ball)

Add a layer of sand to the bucket or bowl. Choose a ball and drop it into the sand from a height of about 50cm (20in). You will see a crater around the ball. Carefully remove the ball so the crater remains intact. Measure the diameter (the width of the crater) and note it down. Draw the crater on the paper. Smooth out the sand and choose another ball. Drop it again from about 50cm (20in), measure the diameter, and draw. Repeat several times with different sizes and types of marbles and balls.

What's happening?

Objects attract each other. The largest object, with the greatest mass, pulls the hardest and makes the smaller (lighter) object move towards it. The earth is the largest mass in our environment and it has a strong pulling force (gravity). This is why objects fall down towards the earth.

Gravity pulls at us too. This is why we are slightly taller in the morning than at night. By night time, gravity has been pulling at us all day long making us a little shorter.

A meteorite is a piece of space debris that may land on earth. Fortunately, our planet is protected by a layer that shields us from meteorites: the atmosphere. Space debris is slowed down by the atmosphere. This causes friction, which in turn burns up most meteorites. That's why it's very rare for a meteorite to make it all the way to the earth.

COMPLICATED... (1)

The conversation between Jesus and Nicodemus JOHN 3

ASK AN ADULT TO HELP YOU!

IT DOESN'T FIT SO IT CAN'T HAPPEN!

You need: peeled hard-boiled egg, glass bottle (with an opening that is slightly narrower than the egg), matches, paper napkin

Does the egg fit through the opening of the bottle? Ask an adult to strike a few matches and drop them carefully into the bottle (or light a piece of rolled up paper napkin or kitchen roll and drop into the bottle for a stronger effect). Quickly place the egg on the opening of the bottle, with the pointy bit down.

Jesus replied, "Very truly I tell you, no one can see the kingdom of God unless they are born again." "How can someone be born when they are old?" Nicodemus asked. "Surely they cannot enter a second time into their mother's womb to be born!"
John 3:3–4

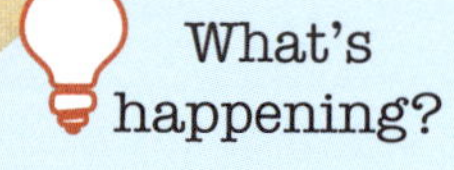

What's happening?

The fire in the bottle uses up oxygen from the air to keep burning. The air pressure in the bottle drops. The air pressure outside the bottle is higher and presses the egg into the bottle

Jesus says that we need to be born again not only physically but also spiritually. What do you think he means?

COMPLICATED... (2)

The conversation between Jesus and Nicodemus JOHN 3

WIND POWER: MAKE AN ORIGAMI PINWHEEL

You need: square piece of paper, scissors, glue, pencil, hammer, nail, stick, yarn, small bead

Fold the paper diagonally across twice, so you get a folded X. Cut along the folds until you're halfway from the middle. Fold over one point of each quarter and glue to the middle. Push the nail through the middle into the stick. Attach the bead to a piece of yarn. Wind the yarn several times around the nail, between the stick and the pinwheel and stick the end of the piece of yarn (without the bead) to the back of the paper. Hold the stick and blow against the pinwheel (sideways). Hold the pinwheel in front of you and start walking slowly. What happens when you start walking faster?

Tip: If your nail is too long and the pinwheel starts flopping, you can thread a bead onto your nail before you join the paper pinwheel to the stick.

"The wind blows wherever it pleases. You hear its sound, but you cannot tell where it comes from or where it is going. So it is with everyone born of the Spirit."
John 3:8

ASK AN ADULT TO HELP YOU.

WIND TURBINES

The wind blows against the blades of wind turbines and they start turning. Inside the turbines a dynamo will start rotating and electricity is generated. There is a magnet inside the dynamo and this magnet is surrounded by electric wire. This wire is made up of electrons, which will start moving when near a magnet. These electrons will start rotating and this movement produces electricity.

There is an electric motor inside a wind turbine. You can test how it works with the following experiment.

ELECTRIC MOTOR

You need: AA battery, small flat magnet, copper wire, small pliers

Bend the wire into the shape seen in the illustration. Place the battery on top of the magnet. Move the copper wire across the battery. What's happening?

ASK AN ADULT TO HELP YOU.

What's happening?

Everywhere around us there is air. Whilst you walk, a current of air will flow past you. When you hold the pinwheel in front of you when walking, the air flow will move the paper of the pinwheel.

THE SECRETS OF GOD'S KINGDOM

Why does Jesus speak in parables? MATTHEW 13

HOMEMADE LOUD SPEAKERS

You need: two paper cups, cardboard tube (kitchen roll tube), kitchen roll, felt tip, scissors, mobile phone

Draw around the bottom end of the mobile phone onto the middle of the cardboard tube. Make a slot: cut the two short sides and one of the long sides and open the flap. Place the end of the tube on the side of a cup (about 1.5cm (½in) from the bottom of the cup) and draw around it. Cut out the circle. Do the same with the other cup. Scrunch up a sheet of kitchen roll and put this in the end of your tube. Repeat at the other end. Push each end of the tube a little way into the hole in each cup. You've made a speaker. Place your mobile phone into the slot in the tube and switch on the music.

The disciples came to him and asked, "Why do you speak to the people in parables?" He replied, "Because the knowledge of the secrets of the kingdom of heaven has been given to you, but not to them. In them is fulfilled the prophecy of Isaiah: 'You will be ever hearing but never understanding; you will be ever seeing but never perceiving. For this people's heart has become calloused; they hardly hear with their ears, and they have closed their eyes. Otherwise they might see with their eyes, hear with their ears, understand with their hearts and turn, and I would heal them.'"

Matthew 13:10–11, 14–15

What's happening?

Sound is made when something is vibrating. The vibrations cause the air to move. These movements are called sound waves. The waves bounce against the walls of the tube and come out again from the cups. The scrunched up kitchen roll absorb the high pitched tones but not the lower tones. This creates a warm sound.

Tip: Add a splash of colour by painting your speaker.

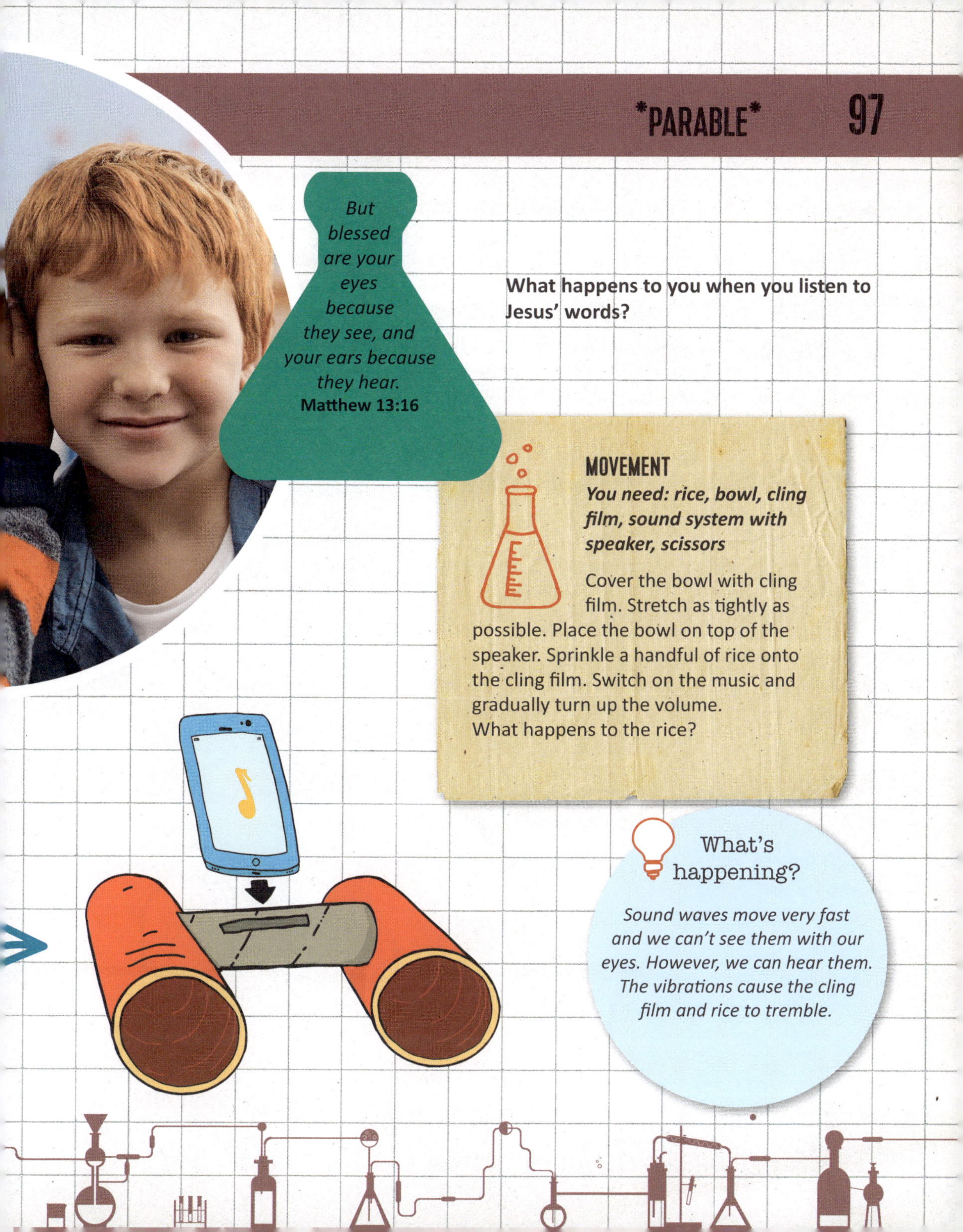

But blessed are your eyes because they see, and your ears because they hear.
Matthew 13:16

What happens to you when you listen to Jesus' words?

MOVEMENT

You need: rice, bowl, cling film, sound system with speaker, scissors

Cover the bowl with cling film. Stretch as tightly as possible. Place the bowl on top of the speaker. Sprinkle a handful of rice onto the cling film. Switch on the music and gradually turn up the volume. What happens to the rice?

What's happening?

Sound waves move very fast and we can't see them with our eyes. However, we can hear them. The vibrations cause the cling film and rice to tremble.

A FIRM FOUNDATION

Parable of the wise and the foolish man LUKE 6

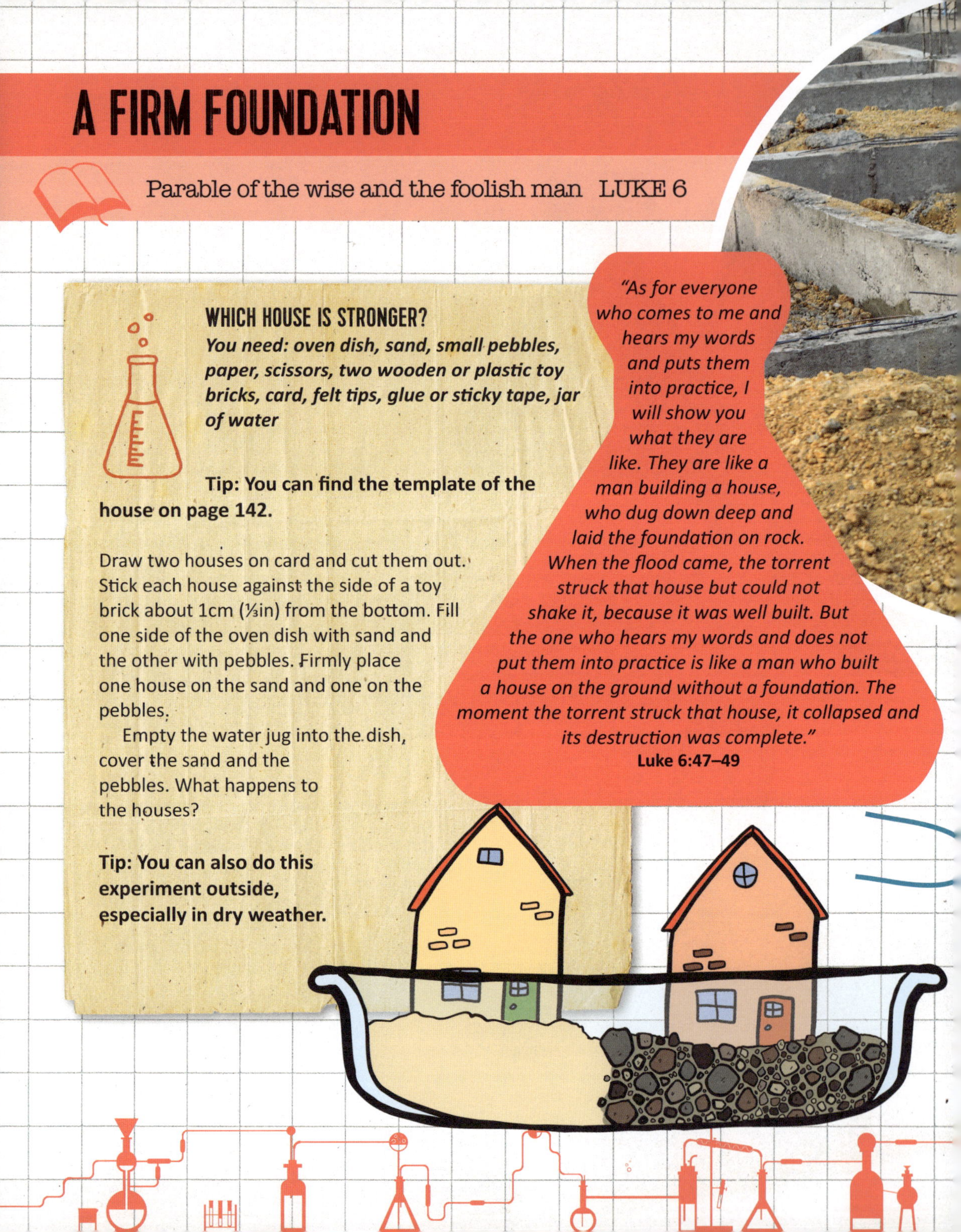

WHICH HOUSE IS STRONGER?

You need: oven dish, sand, small pebbles, paper, scissors, two wooden or plastic toy bricks, card, felt tips, glue or sticky tape, jar of water

Tip: You can find the template of the house on page 142.

Draw two houses on card and cut them out. Stick each house against the side of a toy brick about 1cm (⅓in) from the bottom. Fill one side of the oven dish with sand and the other with pebbles. Firmly place one house on the sand and one on the pebbles.

Empty the water jug into the dish, cover the sand and the pebbles. What happens to the houses?

Tip: You can also do this experiment outside, especially in dry weather.

"As for everyone who comes to me and hears my words and puts them into practice, I will show you what they are like. They are like a man building a house, who dug down deep and laid the foundation on rock. When the flood came, the torrent struck that house but could not shake it, because it was well built. But the one who hears my words and does not put them into practice is like a man who built a house on the ground without a foundation. The moment the torrent struck that house, it collapsed and its destruction was complete."

Luke 6:47–49

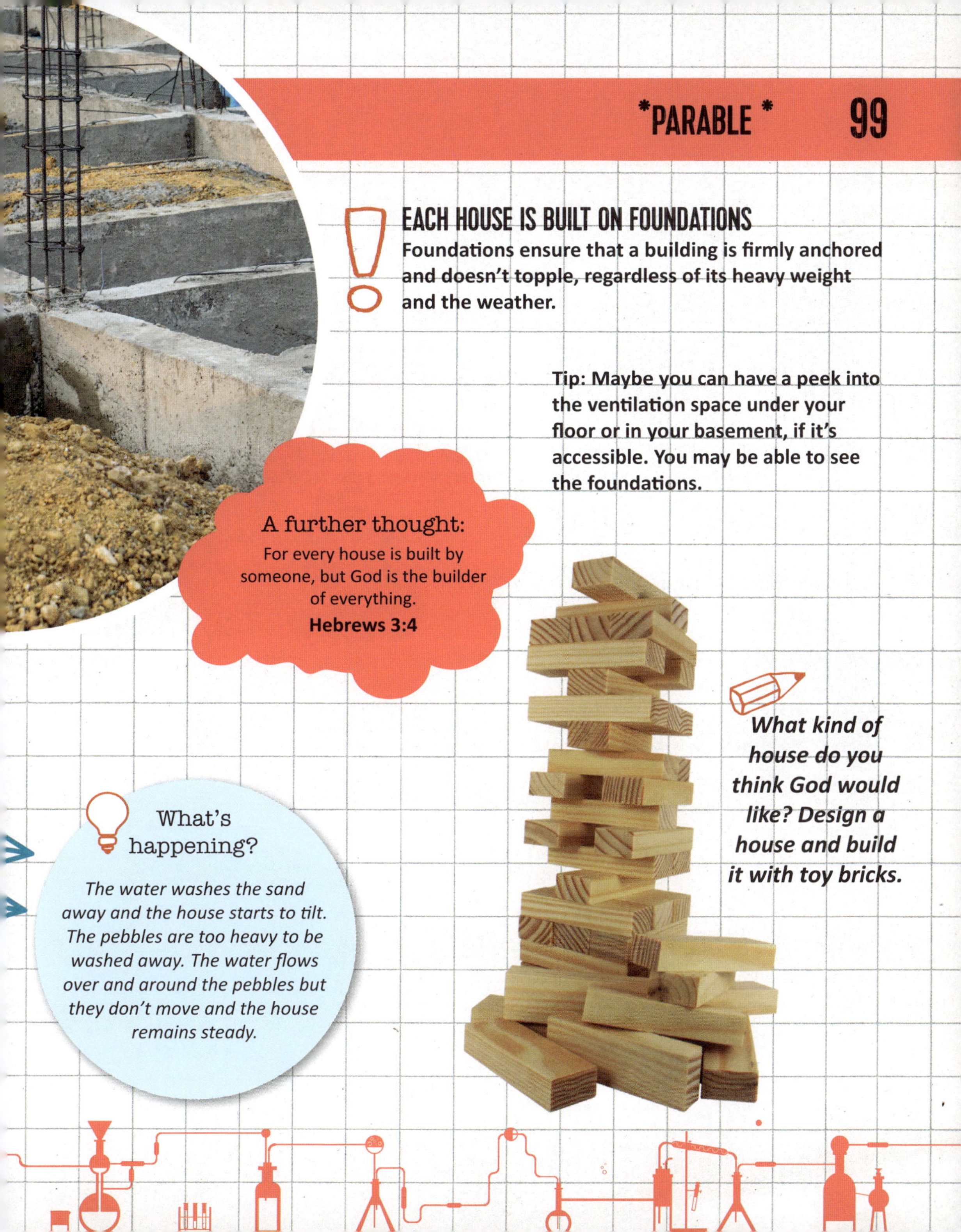

EACH HOUSE IS BUILT ON FOUNDATIONS

Foundations ensure that a building is firmly anchored and doesn't topple, regardless of its heavy weight and the weather.

Tip: Maybe you can have a peek into the ventilation space under your floor or in your basement, if it's accessible. You may be able to see the foundations.

A further thought:

For every house is built by someone, but God is the builder of everything.

Hebrews 3:4

What kind of house do you think God would like? Design a house and build it with toy bricks.

What's happening?

The water washes the sand away and the house starts to tilt. The pebbles are too heavy to be washed away. The water flows over and around the pebbles but they don't move and the house remains steady.

IT GROWS ALL BY ITSELF

Jesus talks about God's kingdom MARK 4

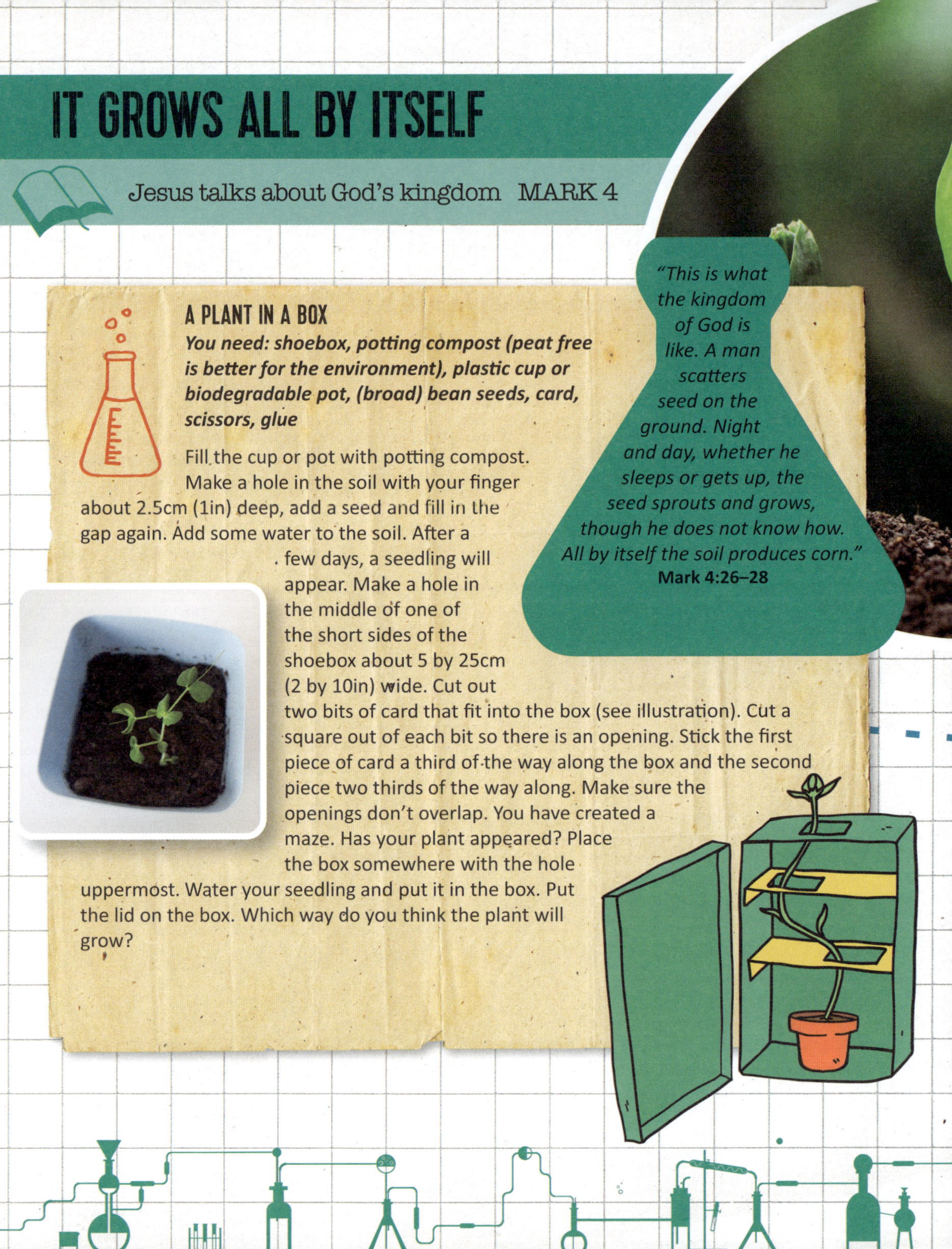

"This is what the kingdom of God is like. A man scatters seed on the ground. Night and day, whether he sleeps or gets up, the seed sprouts and grows, though he does not know how. All by itself the soil produces corn."
Mark 4:26–28

A PLANT IN A BOX

You need: shoebox, potting compost (peat free is better for the environment), plastic cup or biodegradable pot, (broad) bean seeds, card, scissors, glue

Fill the cup or pot with potting compost. Make a hole in the soil with your finger about 2.5cm (1in) deep, add a seed and fill in the gap again. Add some water to the soil. After a few days, a seedling will appear. Make a hole in the middle of one of the short sides of the shoebox about 5 by 25cm (2 by 10in) wide. Cut out two bits of card that fit into the box (see illustration). Cut a square out of each bit so there is an opening. Stick the first piece of card a third of the way along the box and the second piece two thirds of the way along. Make sure the openings don't overlap. You have created a maze. Has your plant appeared? Place the box somewhere with the hole uppermost. Water your seedling and put it in the box. Put the lid on the box. Which way do you think the plant will grow?

"What shall we say the kingdom of God is like, or what parable shall we use to describe it? It is like a mustard seed, which is the smallest of all seeds on earth. Yet when planted, it grows and becomes the largest of all garden plants."
Mark 4:30–32a

What's happening?

A plant needs light to grow. Plant leaves are made up of small green dots called "chloroplasts", which capture sunlight. Light is the plant's energy source to make sugar out of water and carbon dioxide. Plants need sugar to grow. This is why plants always grow towards the light.

Go outside and see what types of tree you can spot. Do you know which seeds (pod) belong to each species?

Tip: There are several apps to identify trees and plants. You can also use a guidebook or identification charts. Have a look at https://www.field-studies-council.org/publications/fold-out-charts.aspx

JESUS TURNS EVERYTHING...

Parable of the workers in the vineyard MATTHEW 20

Read the parable in Matthew 20:1–16.

Jesus' words are not always easy. They may make you happy but can also be challenging. Sometimes Jesus turns everything upside down, just like the story about the owner of the vineyard who is looking for labourers.

So the last will be first, and the first will be last.
Matthew 20:16

UPSIDE DOWN

You need: strong tape, tracing paper or similar, pencil or felt tip, cardboard tube or toilet roll, empty (tissue) box, magnifying glass, pen, scissors

Cut out one side of the box. Place the tube on the opposite side and trace around with a pencil or felt tip. Cut out the circle and push the tube inside. Be careful: you will need to rotate and move the tube back and forth. Stick the magnifying glass onto the other side of the tube (make sure it's firmly attached), so the lens is just in front of the end. Cover the open side of the box with the tracing paper. Point the box with the lens at an object (close up). Something will appear on the tracing paper. What is it?

Tip: If you turn the tube you can focus your image so it's sharp.

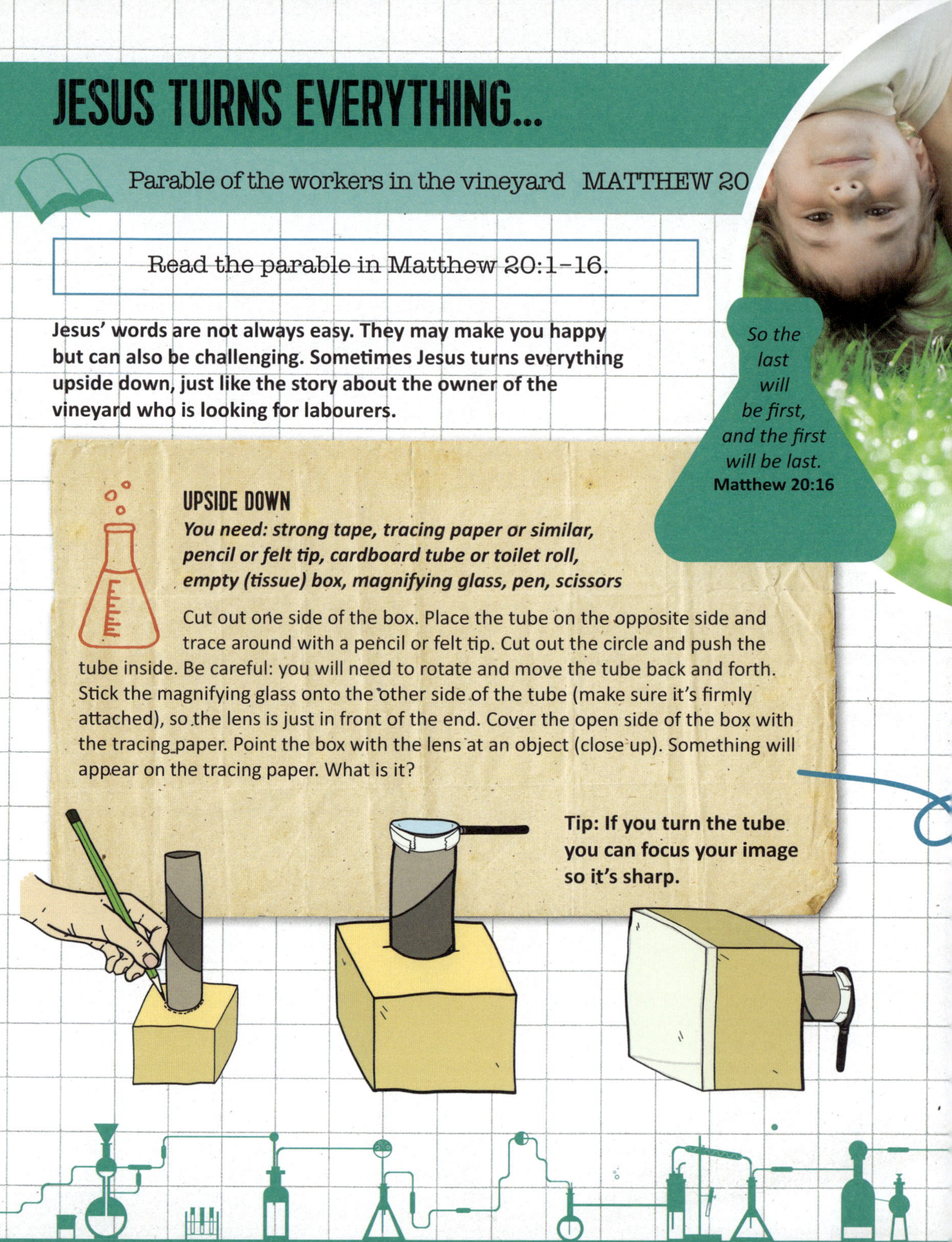

UPSIDE DOWN *PARABLE* 103

EVERYTHING TURNED AROUND

You need: glass, water, paper, felt tip

Draw a horizontal arrow on a piece of paper about 10 by 10cm (4 x 4in)square. Rest the paper against a wall. Put an empty glass in front of the paper about 10cm (4in) away. Look through the glass. What do you see?

Half fill the glass with water and look again. What can you see now?

And what do you see if you move the glass right in front of the piece of paper and then gradually move it away (keep looking through the glass whilst you're moving it)?

Tip: Try this with a square glass. What would you expect to happen?

What's happening?

The water in the glass acts as a spherical lens. If you keep the glass close to the piece of paper with the arrow on, the arrow is enlarged. If you move the glass away, the rays of light can cross one another. And the rays that hit e.g. the tip of the arrow end up on the other side and it's the same for each bit of the image, which turns around completely.

What's happening?

Light is made up of rays, which enable us to see. Rays of light normally move in a straight line, but when they hit a lens, they bend. With a convex (or spherical) lens they bend inwards and with a concave (or hollow) lens, they bend outwards. The magnifying glass has a spherical lens. The rays of light bend inwards and cross before they reach the tracing paper. This way, the image is reversed (we call this a mirror image).

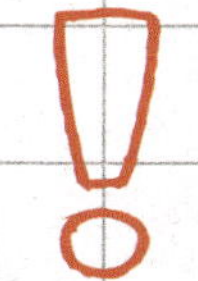

Did you know there is a lens in your eye? Images you see end up on your retina (see page 74), upside down, just as in the experiments. The image is sent to your brain, which will turn it the right way up again.

Read Hannah's song in 1 Samuel 2:1–10 together. Hannah sings about God and how he turns things around for good. Perhaps you can make a list of all the good things that God has done for you?

IN BALANCE

Jesus' miracles MATTHEW 15

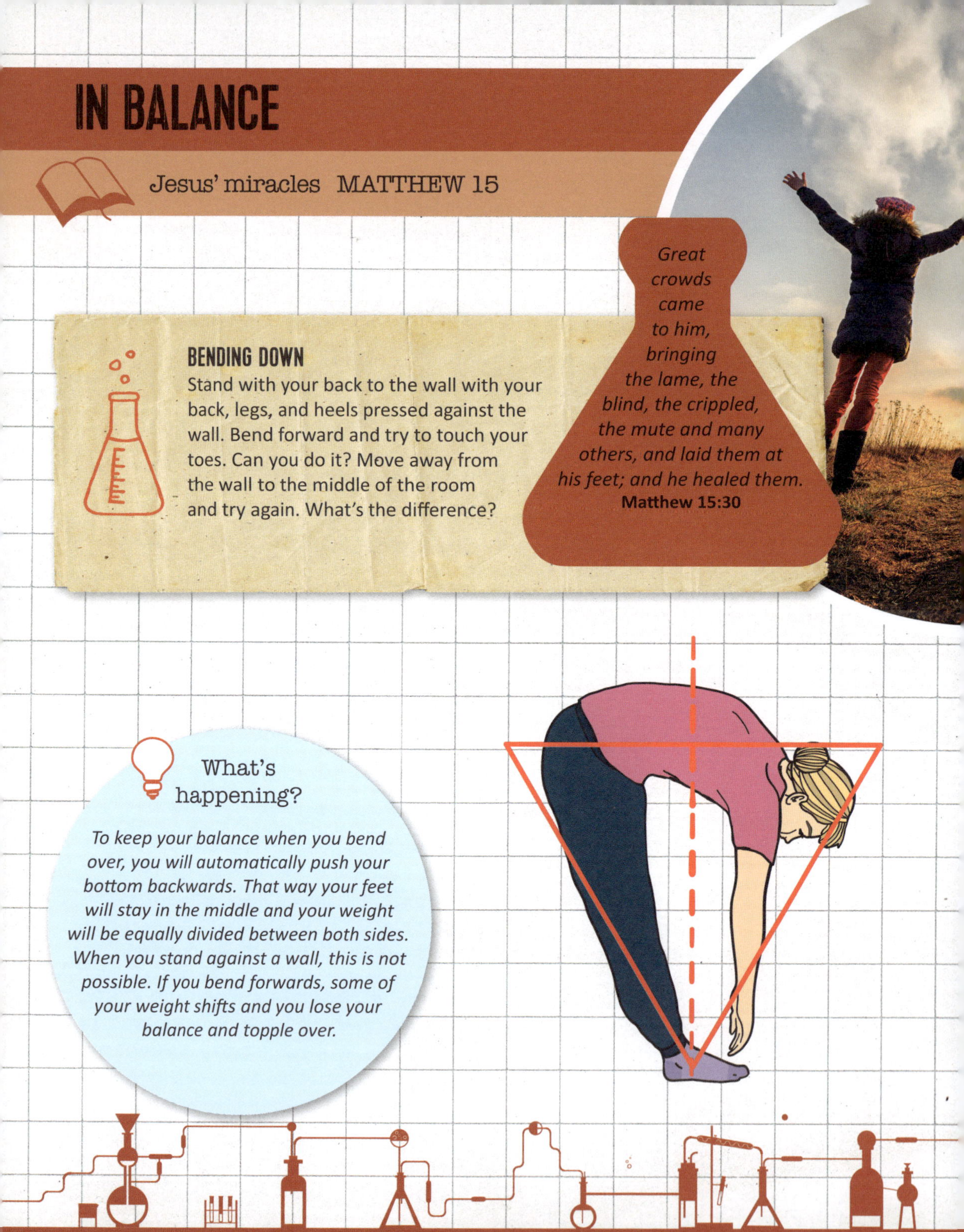

Great crowds came to him, bringing the lame, the blind, the crippled, the mute and many others, and laid them at his feet; and he healed them.
Matthew 15:30

BENDING DOWN

Stand with your back to the wall with your back, legs, and heels pressed against the wall. Bend forward and try to touch your toes. Can you do it? Move away from the wall to the middle of the room and try again. What's the difference?

What's happening?

To keep your balance when you bend over, you will automatically push your bottom backwards. That way your feet will stay in the middle and your weight will be equally divided between both sides. When you stand against a wall, this is not possible. If you bend forwards, some of your weight shifts and you lose your balance and topple over.

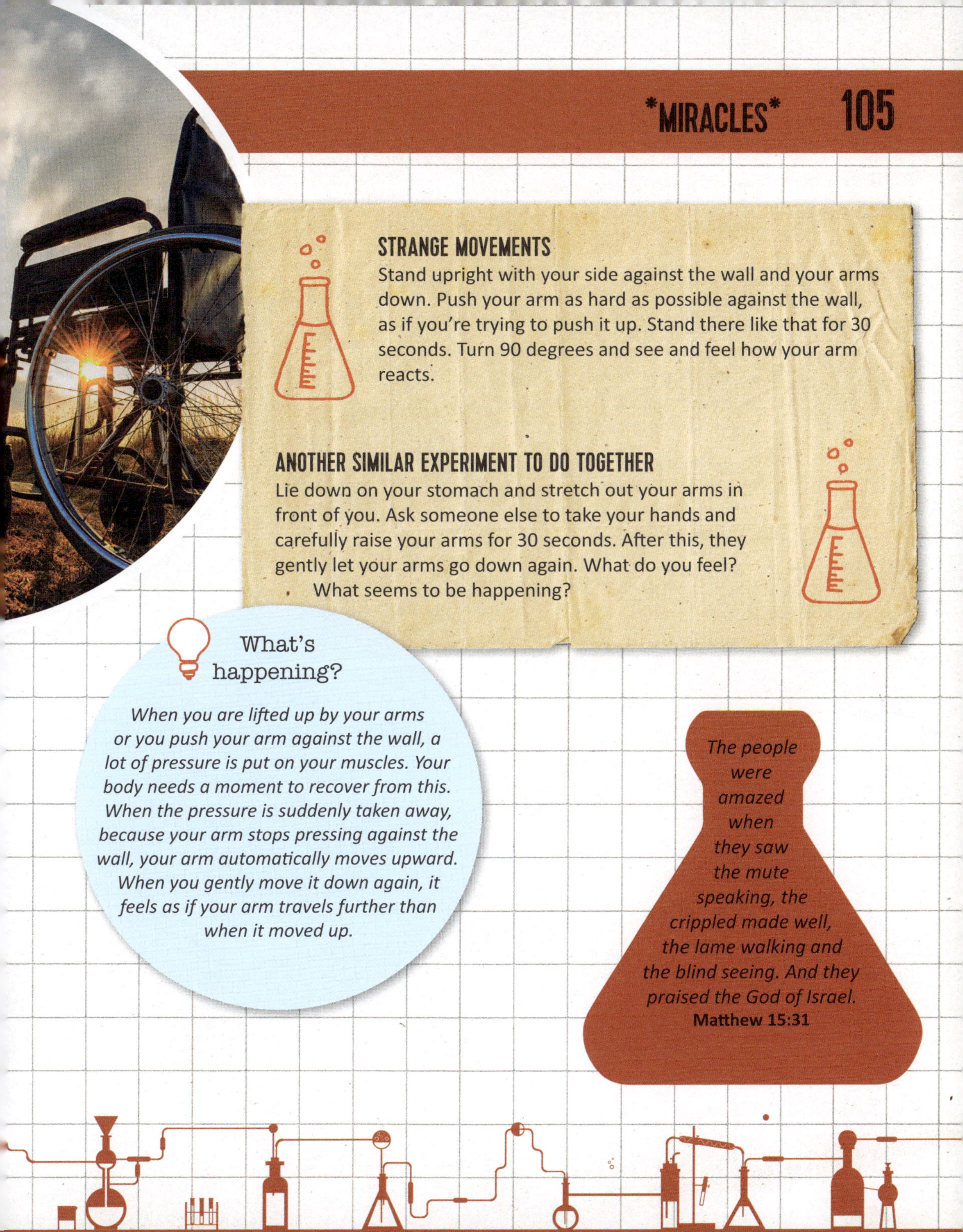

STRANGE MOVEMENTS

Stand upright with your side against the wall and your arms down. Push your arm as hard as possible against the wall, as if you're trying to push it up. Stand there like that for 30 seconds. Turn 90 degrees and see and feel how your arm reacts.

ANOTHER SIMILAR EXPERIMENT TO DO TOGETHER

Lie down on your stomach and stretch out your arms in front of you. Ask someone else to take your hands and carefully raise your arms for 30 seconds. After this, they gently let your arms go down again. What do you feel? What seems to be happening?

What's happening?

When you are lifted up by your arms or you push your arm against the wall, a lot of pressure is put on your muscles. Your body needs a moment to recover from this. When the pressure is suddenly taken away, because your arm stops pressing against the wall, your arm automatically moves upward. When you gently move it down again, it feels as if your arm travels further than when it moved up.

The people were amazed when they saw the mute speaking, the crippled made well, the lame walking and the blind seeing. And they praised the God of Israel.
Matthew 15:31

TRANSFORMING WATER

The wedding in Cana JOHN 2

Jesus said to the servants, "Fill the jars with water"; so they filled them to the brim. Then he told them, "Now draw some out and take it to the master of the banquet."
John 2:7–8

CHANGING COLOUR

You need: red cabbage (chopped), water, blender, sieve, bowl, glass, white vinegar, baking powder and baking soda, teaspoon

Blend the red cabbage and cover it with a little water. Blend again until the mixture is purple. Pour the mixture into the sieve and catch the cabbage juice in a bowl. Quarter fill the glass with cabbage juice and add vinegar until the glass is half full. What happens to the colour of the juice?

Sprinkle on a quarter teaspoon of baking soda. What colour is it now? And finally, sprinkle a quarter teaspoon of baking powder into the glass. You will see that the original colour returns!

Be careful: cabbage juice stains!

And the master of the banquet tasted the water that had been turned into wine. Then he called the bridegroom aside and said, "Everyone brings out the choice wine first and then the cheaper wine after the guests have had too much to drink; but you have saved the best till now."
John 2:9–10

What's happening?

Cabbage juice changes colour if you mix it with either "acids" or "alkalis" (or bases). An acid is an acidic (sour) substance and a base is a bitter one. If you add a base to an acid, the acid changes into a salty substance. Cabbage juice, a base, changes when you add an acid like vinegar. Its colour changes from purple to pinkish red. The mixture also reacts with baking soda; it becomes bluish green. The baking powder is a base. It counters the effect of the acidic vinegar and changes the colour back again.

PALE TEA

You need: water, pan or kettle, glass, mug or cup, teabag, lemon, knife

Make a cup of strong, black tea (no milk). The hot water has absorbed (taken in) the taste and colour of the tea leaves. What colour is the tea? Cut the lemon in quarters and squeeze the lemon juice into the tea. What happens to the colour of the tea? How much lemon juice do you need to get rid of the dark colour?

What's happening?

The citric acid in the lemon juice reacts with the dye in the tea (tannin). It bleaches the tea.

Tea originally comes from China, where people have been drinking tea for thousands of years. It wasn't until about the year 1600 when tea was shipped to Europe. It was very expensive: about £280 per kilo ($370 per 2lbs) in today's money. You could only afford it if you were very wealthy. Later on, when the trade was well established, tea became much cheaper.

CONTAGIOUS

The healing of the leper MARK 1

The man is a leper, he suffers from a skin disease. Nobody dares to go near him, as leprosy is contagious! In biblical times, lepers were very lonely.

Jesus heals the man. He is "clean" again and now he's allowed to mix with other people.

A man with leprosy came to him and begged him on his knees, "If you are willing, you can make me clean." Jesus was indignant. He reached out his hand and touched the man. "I am willing," he said. "Be clean!"
Mark 1:40–42a

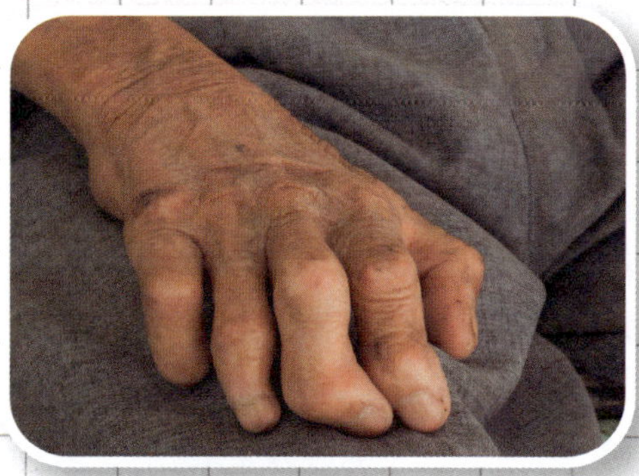

Jesus sent him away at once with a strong warning: "See that you don't tell this to anyone. But go, show yourself to the priest and offer the sacrifices that Moses commanded for your cleansing, as a testimony to them.
Mark 1:43–44

Lepers used to carry a rattle. Whenever they came near other people, they had to announce their presence by making a loud noise with the rattle and shouting "Unclean! Unclean!".

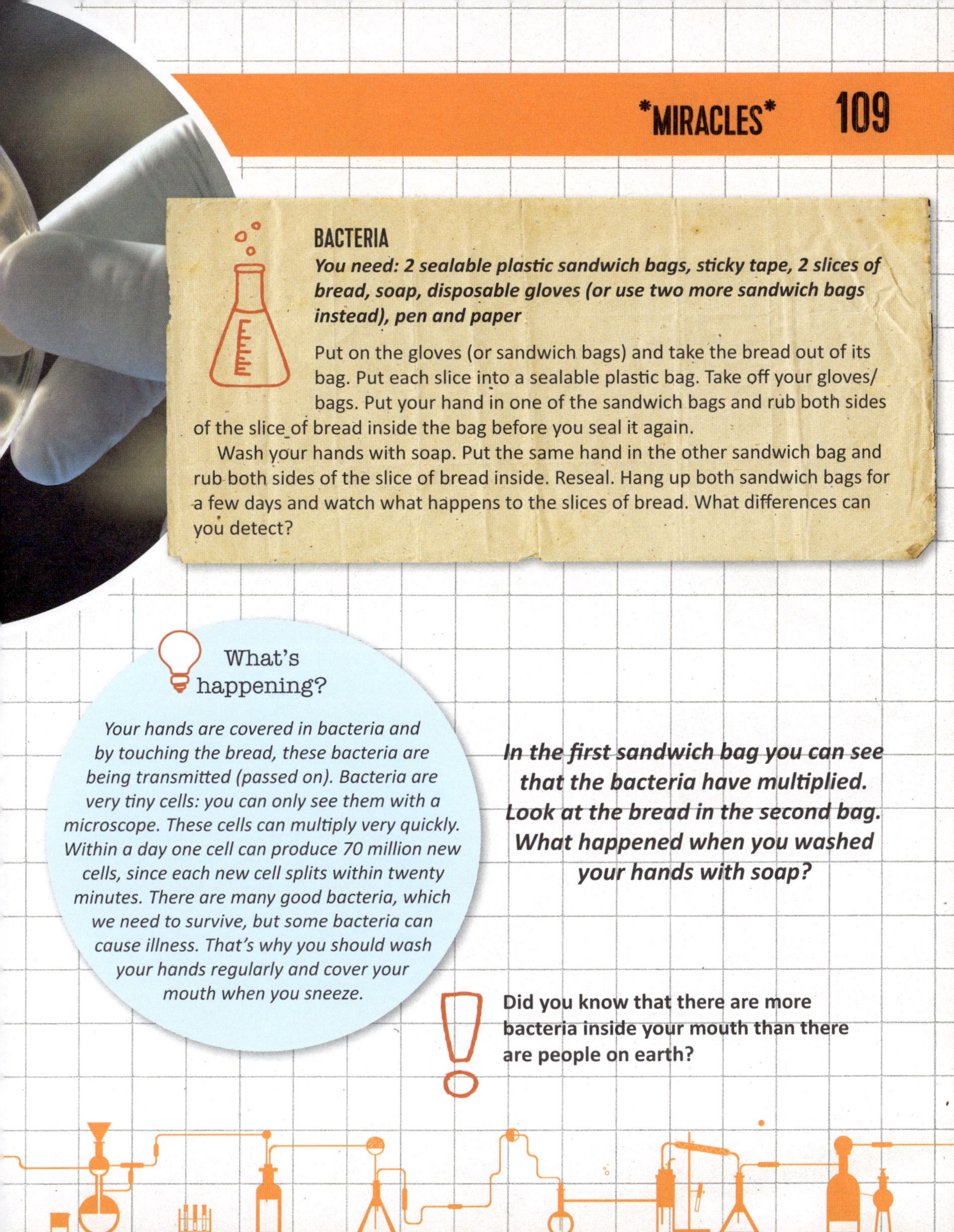

BACTERIA

You need: 2 sealable plastic sandwich bags, sticky tape, 2 slices of bread, soap, disposable gloves (or use two more sandwich bags instead), pen and paper

Put on the gloves (or sandwich bags) and take the bread out of its bag. Put each slice into a sealable plastic bag. Take off your gloves/bags. Put your hand in one of the sandwich bags and rub both sides of the slice of bread inside the bag before you seal it again.

Wash your hands with soap. Put the same hand in the other sandwich bag and rub both sides of the slice of bread inside. Reseal. Hang up both sandwich bags for a few days and watch what happens to the slices of bread. What differences can you detect?

What's happening?

Your hands are covered in bacteria and by touching the bread, these bacteria are being transmitted (passed on). Bacteria are very tiny cells: you can only see them with a microscope. These cells can multiply very quickly. Within a day one cell can produce 70 million new cells, since each new cell splits within twenty minutes. There are many good bacteria, which we need to survive, but some bacteria can cause illness. That's why you should wash your hands regularly and cover your mouth when you sneeze.

In the first sandwich bag you can see that the bacteria have multiplied. Look at the bread in the second bag. What happened when you washed your hands with soap?

Did you know that there are more bacteria inside your mouth than there are people on earth?

STORM ON THE LAKE

Jesus calms the waves and the storm MARK 4

A furious squall came up, and the waves broke over the boat, so that it was nearly swamped. Jesus was in the stern, sleeping on a cushion.
Mark 4:37–38a

SELF-PROPELLED BOAT

You need: baby bath or washing up bowl with water, pencil, paper, scissors, washing up liquid

Trace the template of the boat below onto paper and cut it out (on page 143 you can find a larger template). Place the boat on the water with the back of it against the rim of the bowl or bath.

Add a drop of washing up liquid to the bottom end of the pencil. Touch the water at the back of the boat with the soap on the pencil.

What's happening?

Water is made up of small particles, water molecules. These molecules attract each other and they form a strong layer on the water surface. This is called surface tension. The washing up liquid lowers the surface tension and the molecules start to move. They can only move one way, which is through the opening at the back of the boat. This way, the boat is propelled and moves forward.

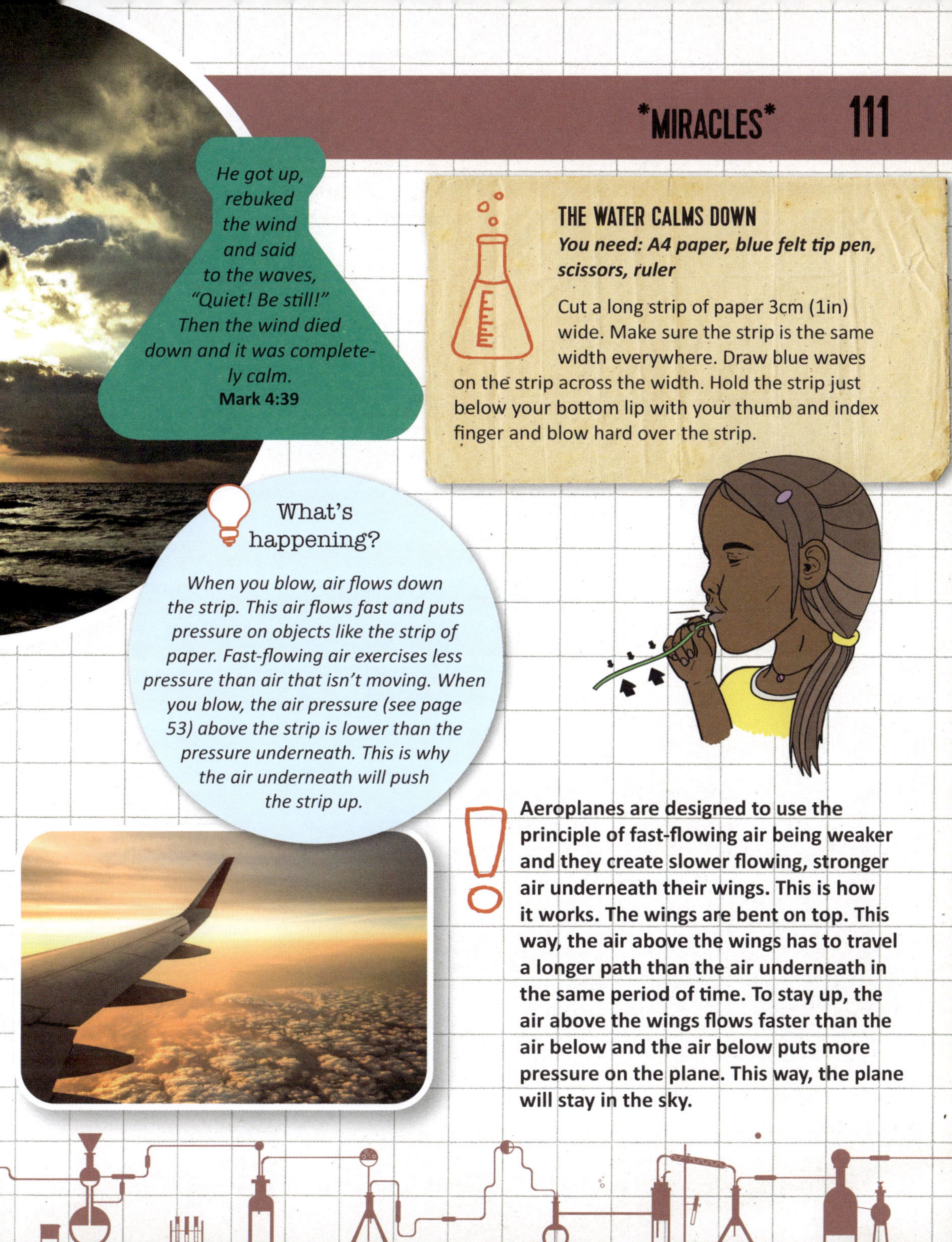

He got up, rebuked the wind and said to the waves, "Quiet! Be still!" Then the wind died down and it was completely calm.
Mark 4:39

THE WATER CALMS DOWN

You need: A4 paper, blue felt tip pen, scissors, ruler

Cut a long strip of paper 3cm (1in) wide. Make sure the strip is the same width everywhere. Draw blue waves on the strip across the width. Hold the strip just below your bottom lip with your thumb and index finger and blow hard over the strip.

What's happening?

When you blow, air flows down the strip. This air flows fast and puts pressure on objects like the strip of paper. Fast-flowing air exercises less pressure than air that isn't moving. When you blow, the air pressure (see page 53) above the strip is lower than the pressure underneath. This is why the air underneath will push the strip up.

Aeroplanes are designed to use the principle of fast-flowing air being weaker and they create slower flowing, stronger air underneath their wings. This is how it works. The wings are bent on top. This way, the air above the wings has to travel a longer path than the air underneath in the same period of time. To stay up, the air above the wings flows faster than the air below and the air below puts more pressure on the plane. This way, the plane will stay in the sky.

SEEING CLEARLY

Healing of the blind man in Bethsaida MARK 8

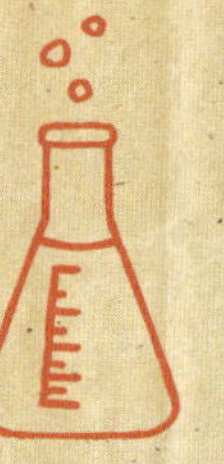

SEEN?

You need: plastic toy bricks of different colours

You need two people for this experiment.

Ask the other person to look at one fixed spot for a while. Choose a toy brick but make sure they don't see it. Slowly move the brick from behind them into their field of vision and ask them to say "stop" as soon as they see the brick. Can they, at this point, tell what colour the brick is?

When he had spat on the man's eyes and put his hands on him, Jesus asked, "Do you see anything?" He looked up and said, "I see people; they look like trees walking around." Once more Jesus put his hands on the man's eyes. Then his eyes were opened, his sight was restored, and he saw everything clearly.

Mark 8:23b–25

What's happening?

When we look at things, our eyes send the image we see to our brain. Our brain adds information to the image, things we already know. This is why we think we can see more than we actually do. If we focus on one spot we think we can see everything else sharply too, just like the image above, but in reality we see it as on the image opposite. We may see something around the edges of the image we are focusing on, but it's not very sharp or accurate. We don't really see any details, such as colours.

Do you need to wear reading glasses? Great, as you can do this experiment!

SEEING WITHOUT GLASSES

You need: pencil with a sharp point, piece of paper

You need someone who uses reading glasses!

Pierce a small hole in the paper with the pencil. Without their glasses on, ask the person to look through the hole at the sentence above with just one eye. They don't need glasses to see the letters clearly!

What's happening?

Light enters our eyes from different directions. In each of our eyes there is a lens. The muscles around the lens enable us to see an image in focus. People who use (reading) glasses can't focus well enough by themselves. When they look through a tiny hole with one eye, the light enters their eye and they focus immediately. Their eye has to adapt less so they can see clearly without needing their glasses.

With your left eye you can never see anything over your right shoulder. And it's the same for your right eye and your left shoulder. Your nose blocks your view. Have a go!

WALKING ON WATER

Jesus and Peter walk on the lake MATTHEW 14

ON THE WATER

You need: glass, water, metal drawing pin (not plastic), washing up liquid

Clean the glass and the drawing pin with water and dry them. Fill the glass with water. Carefully place the pin on the water with the pin uppermost. Does the pin float? The washing up liquid is just like Peter's doubts. Add a small drop of washing up liquid to the water. What happens to the pin?

Shortly before dawn Jesus went out to them, walking on the lake. "Lord, if it's you," Peter replied, "tell me to come to you on the water." "Come," he said. Then Peter got down out of the boat, walked on the water and came towards Jesus.
Matthew 14:25, 28–29

But when he saw the wind, he was afraid and, beginning to sink, cried out, "Lord, save me!" Immediately Jesus reached out his hand and caught him. "You of little faith," he said, "why did you doubt?"
Matthew 14:30– 31

What's happening?

The smallest particles in water are called water molecules. Water molecules attract one another and form a strong layer on the water surface. This layer is also called surface tension. The drawing pin will float on this layer. The washing up liquid destroys the surface tension and the drawing pin can no longer float.

A further thought:

But when you ask, you must believe and not doubt, because the one who doubts is like a wave of the sea, blown and tossed by the wind.
James 1:6

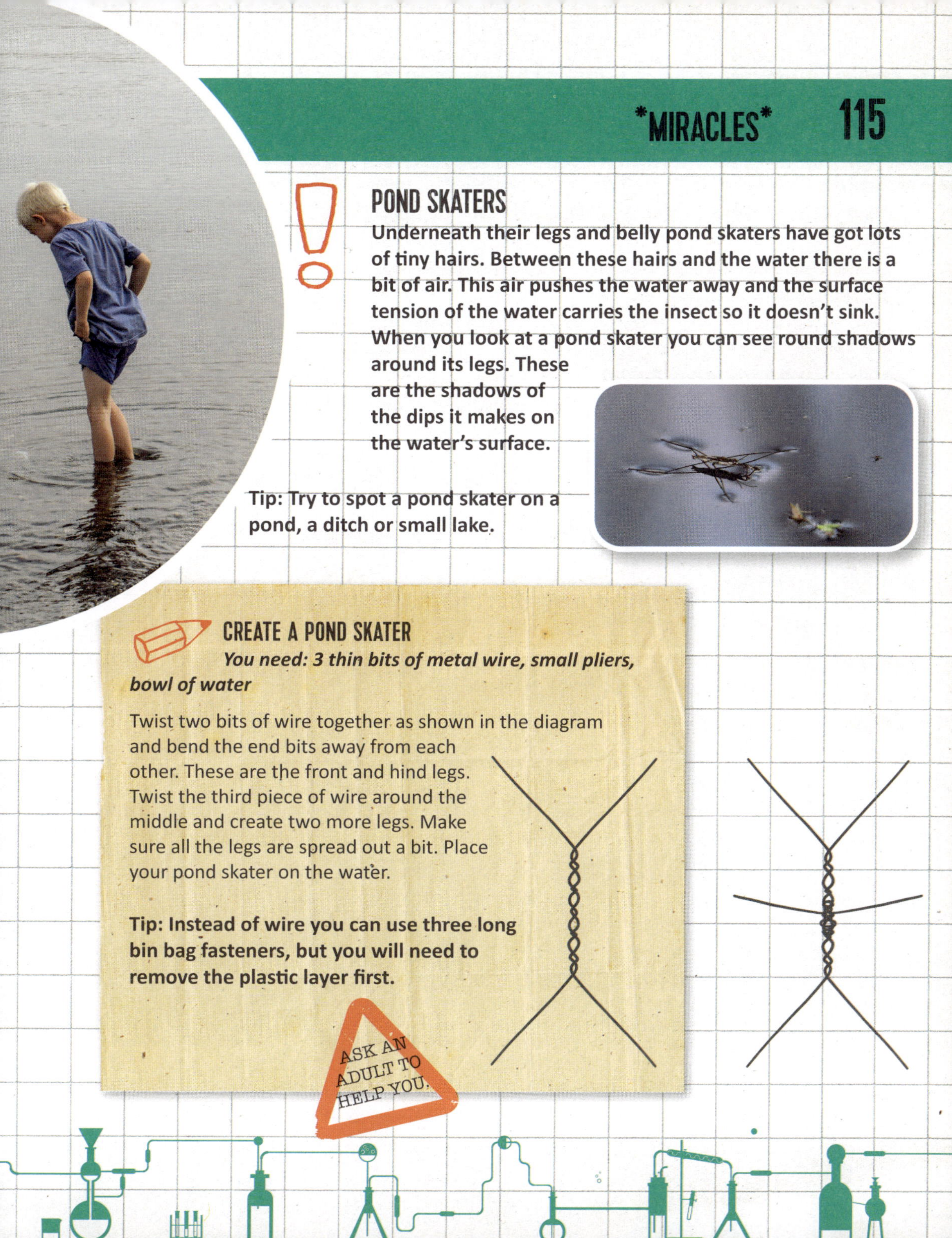

POND SKATERS

Underneath their legs and belly pond skaters have got lots of tiny hairs. Between these hairs and the water there is a bit of air. This air pushes the water away and the surface tension of the water carries the insect so it doesn't sink. When you look at a pond skater you can see round shadows around its legs. These are the shadows of the dips it makes on the water's surface.

Tip: Try to spot a pond skater on a pond, a ditch or small lake.

CREATE A POND SKATER

You need: 3 thin bits of metal wire, small pliers, bowl of water

Twist two bits of wire together as shown in the diagram and bend the end bits away from each other. These are the front and hind legs. Twist the third piece of wire around the middle and create two more legs. Make sure all the legs are spread out a bit. Place your pond skater on the water.

Tip: Instead of wire you can use three long bin bag fasteners, but you will need to remove the plastic layer first.

A VERY DARK DAY

Jesus dies at Golgotha MARK 15

The day when Jesus died on the cross seems a dark, pitch-black day. How black is the colour black do you think?

They brought Jesus to the place called Golgotha (which means "the place of the skull"). And they crucified him. Dividing up his clothes, they cast lots to see what each would get. At noon, darkness came over the whole land until three in the afternoon. And at three in the afternoon Jesus cried out in a loud voice, "Eloi, Eloi, lema sabachthani?" (which means "My God, my God, why have you forsaken me?").
Mark 15:22, 24, 33–34

IS BLACK REALLY BLACK?

You need: glass containing a little water, white (coffee) filter paper, cocktail stick, black felt tip or water-soluble marker pen

Cut a strip from the filter paper. Draw a thick black cross about 1cm (⅓in) away from the bottom edge. Push the cocktail stick through the top end and hang the strip in the glass. Be careful: the water must touch the bottom bit of the strip but not the black cross.

The strip will slowly absorb the water. What happens to the black cross?

What's happening?

Light consists of many different colours all put together. Which colour you see depends on which part of the light is reflected. Black isn't a real colour. Black is a lack of light. Because black isn't a colour, you can't make black colouring. How are black felt tips or paints made? You mix colours! If you mix red, green, and blue you will almost get black.

With a loud cry, Jesus breathed his last.
Mark 15:37

Mixing light

Mixing paint

COLOUR!

You need: small dish, milk, food colouring (red, blue, green, yellow), cotton bud, washing up liquid

Fill the dish with milk and add a drop of blue, yellow, and green food colouring (or three other colours except red). After this, add a drop of red food colouring, which has to sit on top of the other colours. Dip the cotton bud into the washing up liquid. Carefully touch the red food colouring. Repeat a few times.

What's happening?

The smallest water particles are called water molecules. Water molecules attract each other and form a strong layer. This layer is called "surface tension". The food colouring floats thanks to the water's surface tension. The washing up liquid destroys this layer and the food colouring will flow towards the area where the layer is still stronger; this is as far away from the washing up liquid as possible.

The story of Jesus' death is not the end, but the beginning! Read Mark 16:1–6 (and the rest of the chapter).

After Good Friday it is Easter. Jesus has risen! Colour has reappeared in the dark world.

SIN? JESUS PAYS THE PRICE!

Jesus dies for our sins MARK 10

EASILY "INCENSED"

You need: candle on a stand, matches

Ask an adult to light a candle. Leave it to burn for a while and then blow it out. Light another match. What happens if you hold a burning match in the candle smoke?

"For even the Son of Man did not come to be served, but to serve, and to give his life as a ransom for many."
Mark 10:45

What's happening?

Just after you've blown out the candle, the candle wax is hot enough to evaporate (turn to vapour). The wax vapour that rises with the smoke is flammable and will be lit again by the match.

All of us can be "fiery" or easily "incensed". All of a sudden, you may flare up in anger or do something wrong. Jesus wants to forgive us every time this happens.

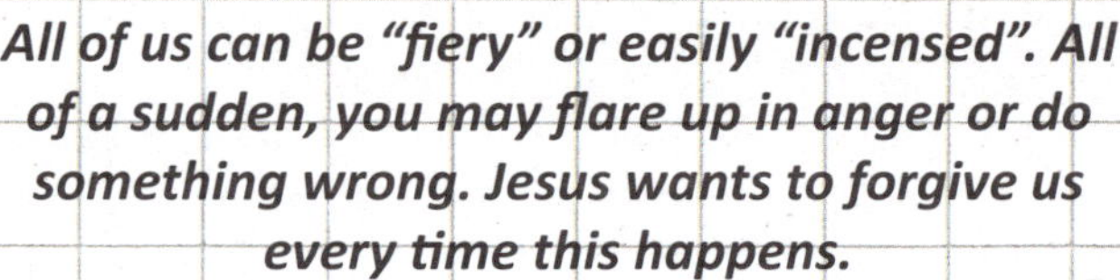

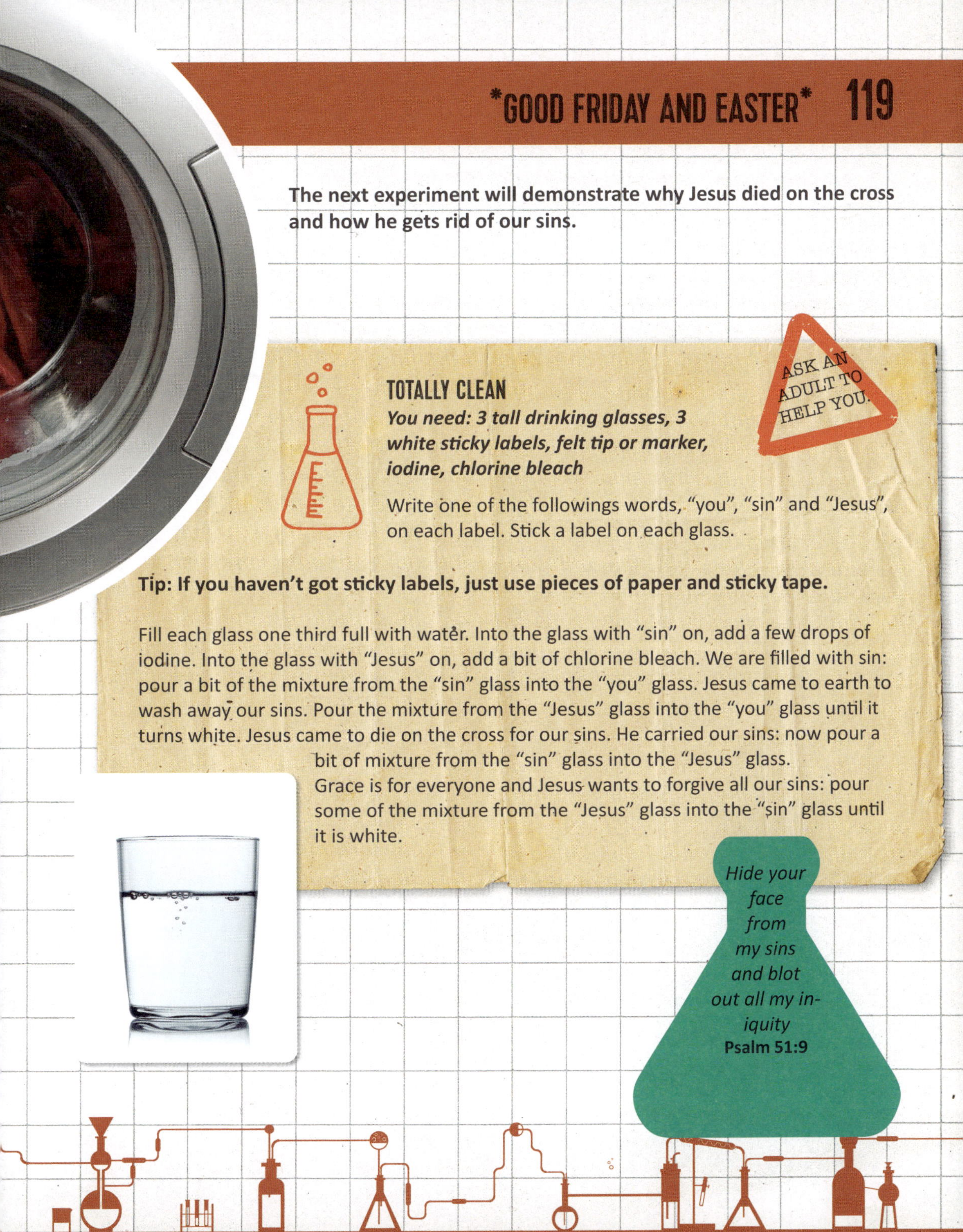

The next experiment will demonstrate why Jesus died on the cross and how he gets rid of our sins.

ASK AN ADULT TO HELP YOU.

TOTALLY CLEAN

You need: 3 tall drinking glasses, 3 white sticky labels, felt tip or marker, iodine, chlorine bleach

Write one of the followings words, "you", "sin" and "Jesus", on each label. Stick a label on each glass.

Tip: If you haven't got sticky labels, just use pieces of paper and sticky tape.

Fill each glass one third full with water. Into the glass with "sin" on, add a few drops of iodine. Into the glass with "Jesus" on, add a bit of chlorine bleach. We are filled with sin: pour a bit of the mixture from the "sin" glass into the "you" glass. Jesus came to earth to wash away our sins. Pour the mixture from the "Jesus" glass into the "you" glass until it turns white. Jesus came to die on the cross for our sins. He carried our sins: now pour a bit of mixture from the "sin" glass into the "Jesus" glass.
Grace is for everyone and Jesus wants to forgive all our sins: pour some of the mixture from the "Jesus" glass into the "sin" glass until it is white.

Hide your face from my sins and blot out all my iniquity
Psalm 51:9

LOVE WARMS YOU UP!

God's love for the world JOHN 3

For God so loved the world that he gave his one and only Son, that whoever believes in him shall not perish but have eternal life.
John 3:16

IT'S GETTING WARM!

You need: 2 glasses, water, thermometer (use either a simple one or a digital one), pen, 2 strips of paper, tablespoon, calcium chloride (a salt you can get as little sachets that absorb moisture)

Be careful! Calcium chloride can cause irritation. Make sure you avoid getting it in your eyes, but if you do, rinse thoroughly with water. Wash your hands and all equipment you have used with soap and water.

Fill each glass two thirds full with cold water. Place a strip of paper underneath each glass. Measure the water temperature and write it on the strip of paper. Add two tablespoons of calcium chloride to one of the glasses and mark the relevant strip with a "C". Measure the temperature of the water in both glasses again.

ASK AN ADULT TO HELP YOU.

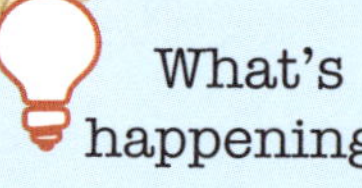

What's happening?

Calcium chloride and water react when mixed. In the process, energy is released in the form of heat and the water temperature rises. When heat is produced during an experiment with different substances we talk about an "exothermic reaction".

A new command I give you: love one another. As I have loved you, so you must love one another.
John 13:34

You can compare love with calcium chloride: it warms us up from the inside, but it can also warm up others. Wrap your hands around the glass – what do you feel?

HEAT CAUSES MOTION

You need: paper, scissors, pencil, piece of string

Cut a spiral shape out of the paper, just as in the picture below. Pierce a hole in the middle and attach the string. Hang the spiral above a radiator.

Tip: Before you cut the spiral, you can colour in the circle using different colours or you can use patterned paper for the circle.

What's happening?

The radiator heats up the air above it. The warm air rises and sets the spiral in motion.

Calcium chloride is used in grit (or de-icing salt) to make ice and snow on the roads melt more quickly.

NEW LIFE

Jesus has risen! MATTHEW 28

Read the Easter story.

There was a violent earthquake, for an angel of the Lord came down from heaven and, going to the tomb, rolled back the stone and sat on it.
Matthew 28:2

HOW STRONG IS NEW LIFE?

You need: 15 dried (kidney or runner) beans, plastic cup, little dish or plate, plaster of Paris (a craft material)

Prepare a little of plaster of Paris mixture (use the instructions on the pack). Mix the beans with the mixture and pour it into the plastic cup. Leave to dry. When dry, carefully remove the mixture from the plastic cup and place on the dish. Make sure the plaster doesn't dry out too much. You can add a bit of water. Be patient for a few days... What can you see?

The angel said to the women, "Do not be afraid, for I know that you are looking for Jesus, who was crucified. He is not here; he has risen, just as he said. Come and see the place where he lay."
Matthew 28:5–6

What's happening?

Plants are very strong! The plaster contains tiny holes and cracks. The bean will burst open and small roots will begin to grow and try to find space. They creep into the small holes and start growing. Very gradually, the plaster will split and tear apart.

A further thought:

When you sow, you do not plant the body that will be, but just a seed, perhaps of wheat or of something else. But God gives it a body as he has determined, and to each kind of seed he gives its own body.
1 Corinthians 15:37–38

Sometimes the tarmac is torn up or paving stones are lifted near trees. This is because the tree roots have been pushing up the tarmac or stones from underneath.

JESUS ASCENDS...

Ascension ACTS 1

WE CAN'T SEE THE WHOLE PICTURE

You need: 3D glasses (with red and blue lenses), mirror

We can't see all of God's plans for the world and for when Jesus returns. It's a bit like the following experiment.

Look in the mirror with the 3D glasses on. Close your left eye and look in the mirror with your right eye. What can you see? Close your right eye and look in the mirror with your left eye. What is the difference?

Then they gathered round him and asked him, "Lord, are you at this time going to restore the kingdom to Israel?" He said to them: "It is not for you to know the times or dates the Father has set by his own authority."

Acts 1:6–7

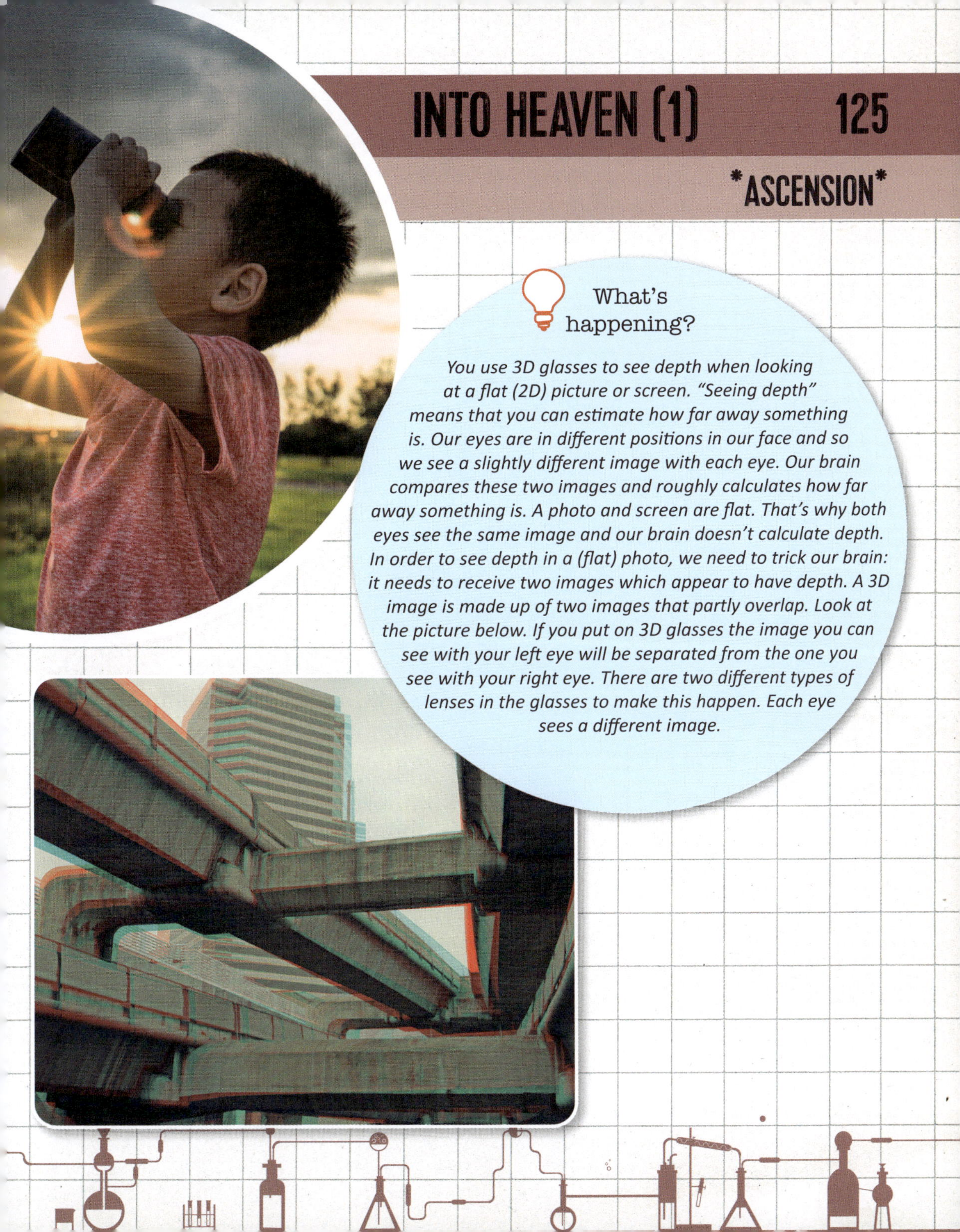

ASCENSION

What's happening?

You use 3D glasses to see depth when looking at a flat (2D) picture or screen. "Seeing depth" means that you can estimate how far away something is. Our eyes are in different positions in our face and so we see a slightly different image with each eye. Our brain compares these two images and roughly calculates how far away something is. A photo and screen are flat. That's why both eyes see the same image and our brain doesn't calculate depth. In order to see depth in a (flat) photo, we need to trick our brain: it needs to receive two images which appear to have depth. A 3D image is made up of two images that partly overlap. Look at the picture below. If you put on 3D glasses the image you can see with your left eye will be separated from the one you see with your right eye. There are two different types of lenses in the glasses to make this happen. Each eye sees a different image.

JESUS ASCENDS...

Ascension ACTS 1

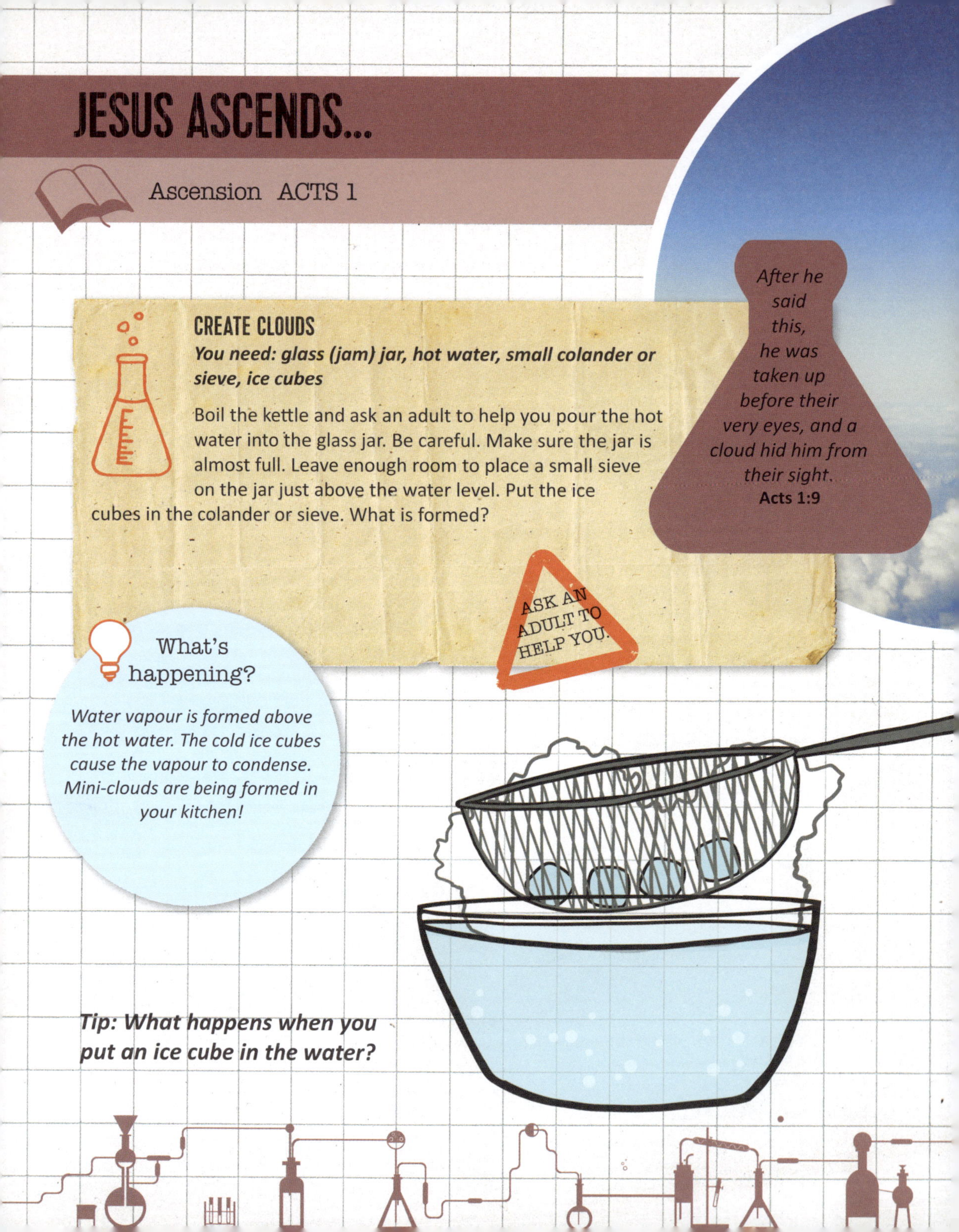

CREATE CLOUDS

You need: glass (jam) jar, hot water, small colander or sieve, ice cubes

Boil the kettle and ask an adult to help you pour the hot water into the glass jar. Be careful. Make sure the jar is almost full. Leave enough room to place a small sieve on the jar just above the water level. Put the ice cubes in the colander or sieve. What is formed?

After he said this, he was taken up before their very eyes, and a cloud hid him from their sight.
Acts 1:9

What's happening?

Water vapour is formed above the hot water. The cold ice cubes cause the vapour to condense. Mini-clouds are being formed in your kitchen!

Tip: What happens when you put an ice cube in the water?

ASCENSION

They were looking intently up into the sky as he was going, when suddenly two men dressed in white stood beside them. "Men of Galilee," they said, "why do you stand here looking into the sky? This same Jesus, who has been taken from you into heaven, will come back in the same way you have seen him go into heaven."

Acts 1:10–11

MINI-ROCKETS

You need: empty container with a push-on lid (such as a play-dough tub), effervescent tablets (any type), water. You may like to do this outside!

Pour 1cm (⅓in) of water in the canister or pot. Add a tablet and quickly put the lid on. Briefly shake the pot and put it on the ground upside down. Quickly take a step back and watch...

ON THE MOVE!

The outpouring of the Holy Spirit ACTS 2

DANCING RAISINS

You need: sparkling (carbonated) water, raisins, glass

Fill the glass with sparkling water. Add the raisins. What can you see?

Suddenly a sound like the blowing of a violent wind came from heaven and filled the whole house where they were sitting. They saw what seemed to be tongues of fire that separated and came to rest on each of them. All of them were filled with the Holy Spirit and began to speak in other tongues as the Spirit enabled them.

Acts 2:2–4

What's happening?

Sparkling water contains carbon dioxide, a gas. As soon as you open the bottle and pour yourself a glass, the carbon dioxide will evaporate (turn to vapour). The little bubbles are carbon dioxide bubbles. The bubbles will cling to the raisins. The bubbles rise and take the small raisins with them, as they are light enough to be carried. As soon as the bubbles reach the surface however, they let go of the raisin, which will sink to the bottom. The carbon dioxide gas ends up in the air.

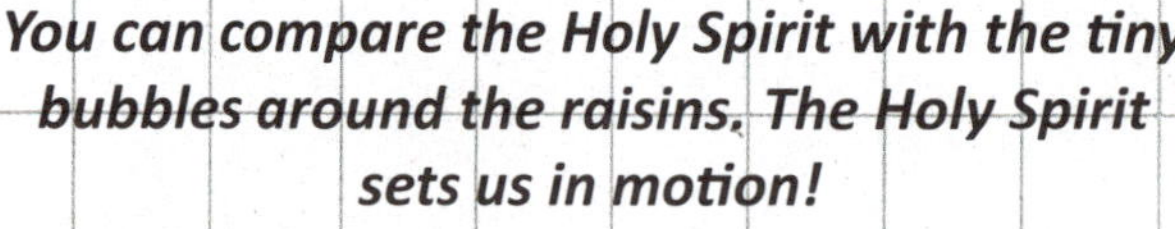

You can compare the Holy Spirit with the tiny bubbles around the raisins. The Holy Spirit sets us in motion!

FIZZING

You need: cola, salt, spoon, glass

Half fill the glass with cola. Add a spoonful of salt.

What's happening?

Cola contains dissolved carbon dioxide too. When you pour cola in a glass, the gas is released and will form small air bubbles. The bubbles will attach themselves to a grain of salt. As there are so many salt grains in the glass, you will see a lot of bubbles. The carbon dioxide gas ends up in the air.

A further thought:

Jesus said: "You are the salt of the earth."
Matthew 5:13a

THE POWER OF GOD

The Holy Spirit ROMANS 5

The Holy Spirit, who came into the world at Pentecost, filled Jesus' disciples. The Spirit made them strong and courageous. They told everyone who was willing to listen about Jesus. The same Spirit has been given to you too. Christians often say that the Spirit lives in their heart. What do you think that means?

And hope does not put us to shame, because God's love has been poured out into our hearts through the Holy Spirit, who has been given to us.
Romans 5:5

HIDDEN POWER

You need: 150g (5oz) of a breakfast cereal fortified with iron (such as Special K®), measuring jug, large bowl or dish, serving spoon, water, strong magnet, hand blender, white or transparent latex glove

Pour the cereal into the bowl. Crumble the flakes and crush them with the spoon. Add 1 litre (33fl oz) of water, stir, and leave for 5 minutes. Blend the flakes and water with the hand blender. Fill the measuring jug with water. Put the magnet in the latex glove and fold the glove tightly around it. Stir the cereal mixture with the glove containing the magnet, moving it round the bottom of the bowl. Next, immerse (soak) the glove in the jug of water. What can you see?

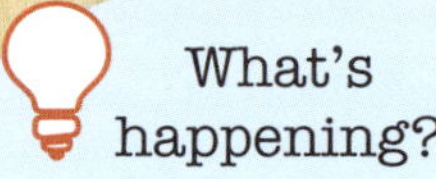

What's happening?

Tiny pieces of iron are added to Special K® and similar breakfast cereals. When you crumble the flakes and soak them in water, the bits of iron will detach themselves from the flakes. The magnet collects the bits of iron in the mixture, which you can see when you put the glove and magnet into the jug of water.

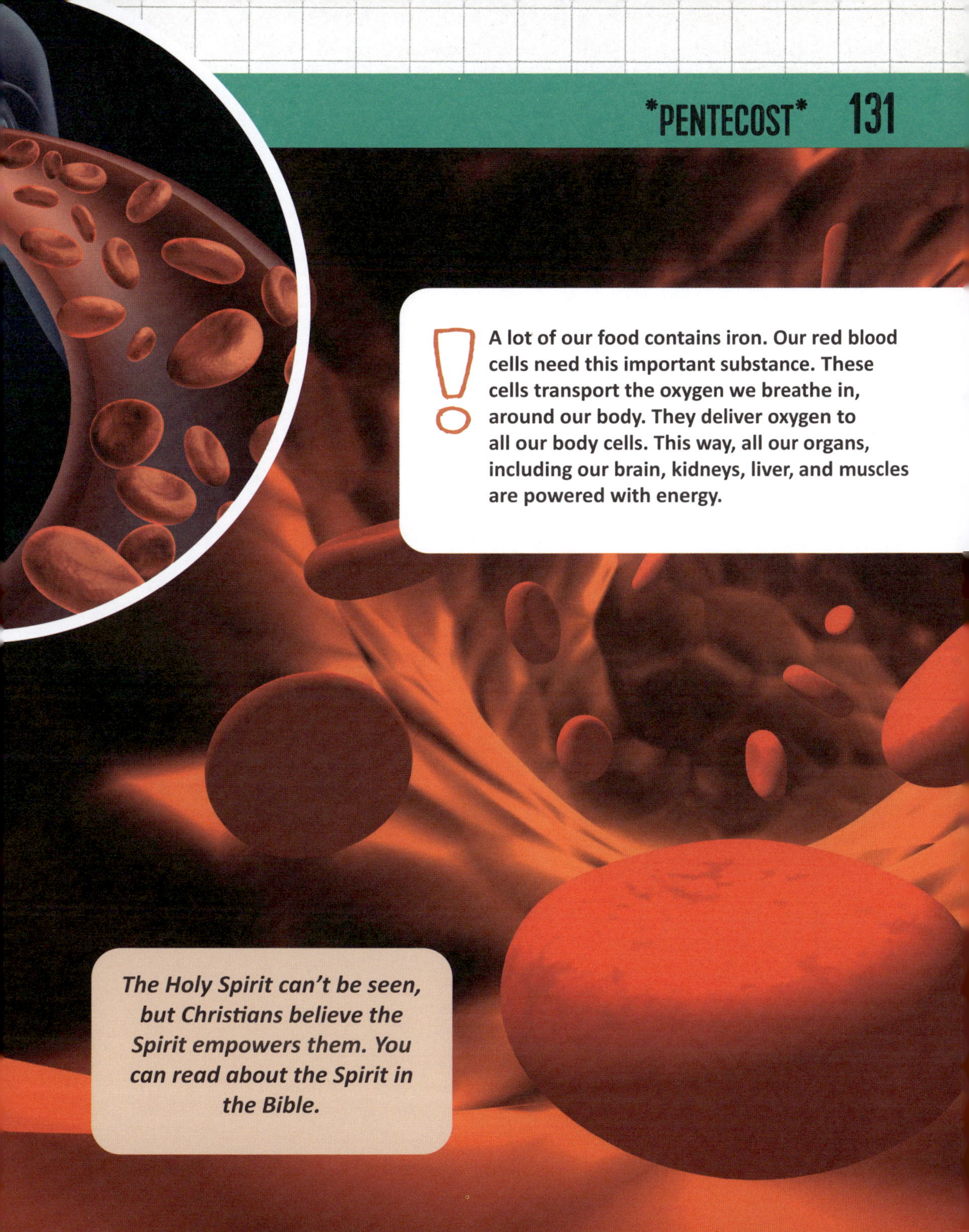

A lot of our food contains iron. Our red blood cells need this important substance. These cells transport the oxygen we breathe in, around our body. They deliver oxygen to all our body cells. This way, all our organs, including our brain, kidneys, liver, and muscles are powered with energy.

The Holy Spirit can't be seen, but Christians believe the Spirit empowers them. You can read about the Spirit in the Bible.

READ IT IN THE BIBLE

Philip and the Ethiopian ACTS 8

DO YOU UNDERSTAND WHAT YOU HEAR?

You need: drawing pin or other pin, pencil, disposable plastic cup, string the length of your arm, kitchen towel, water

Use the pin to pierce a hole in the bottom of the cup. You can use the pencil tip to make the hole bigger. Make a thick knot in one end of the string. Push the end of string without the knot through the hole in the cup from the inside and make another knot. Put some water on the piece of kitchen paper. Lift up the cup with one hand and, with your other hand, fold the damp paper around the string and pull it down. What can you hear? What does the noise sound like?

Then Philip ran up to the chariot and heard the man reading Isaiah the prophet. "Do you understand what you are reading?" Philip asked. "How can I," he said, "unless someone explains it to me?" So he invited Philip to come up and sit with him.

Acts 8:30–31

What's happening?

When you move the wet piece of kitchen towel up and down the string, the string will start to vibrate. The plastic cup will start to vibrate too. The cup acts as a loud speaker and amplifies the sound.

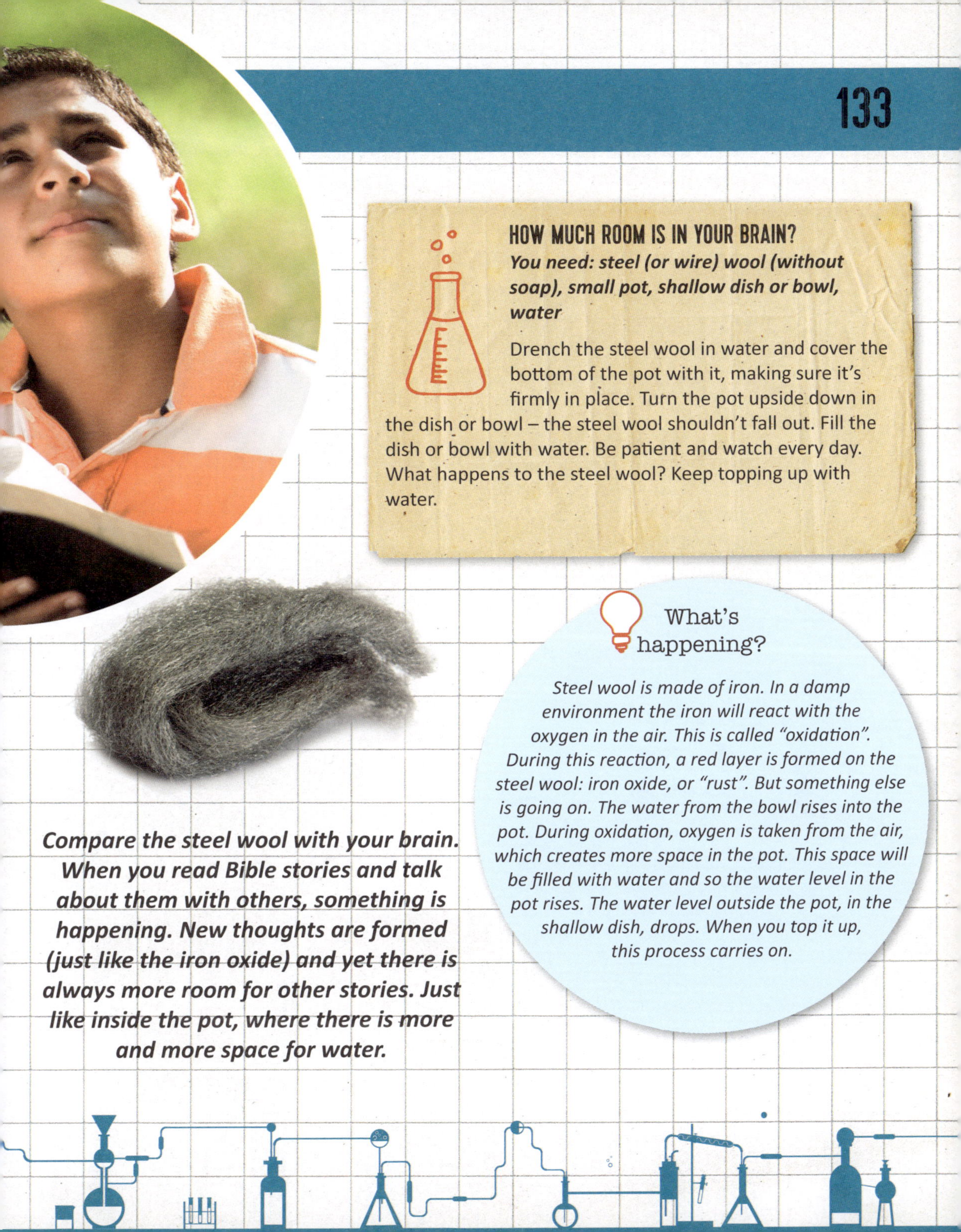

HOW MUCH ROOM IS IN YOUR BRAIN?

You need: steel (or wire) wool (without soap), small pot, shallow dish or bowl, water

Drench the steel wool in water and cover the bottom of the pot with it, making sure it's firmly in place. Turn the pot upside down in the dish or bowl – the steel wool shouldn't fall out. Fill the dish or bowl with water. Be patient and watch every day. What happens to the steel wool? Keep topping up with water.

Compare the steel wool with your brain. When you read Bible stories and talk about them with others, something is happening. New thoughts are formed (just like the iron oxide) and yet there is always more room for other stories. Just like inside the pot, where there is more and more space for water.

What's happening?

Steel wool is made of iron. In a damp environment the iron will react with the oxygen in the air. This is called "oxidation". During this reaction, a red layer is formed on the steel wool: iron oxide, or "rust". But something else is going on. The water from the bowl rises into the pot. During oxidation, oxygen is taken from the air, which creates more space in the pot. This space will be filled with water and so the water level in the pot rises. The water level outside the pot, in the shallow dish, drops. When you top it up, this process carries on.

JESUS TRANSFORMS FIERCE SAUL

Saul's conversion ACTS 9

Meanwhile, Saul was still breathing out murderous threats against the Lord's disciples.
Acts 9:1a

A BOLT OF LIGHTNING

You need: metal cake slice, glass, piece of polystyrene or plastic foam, woollen jumper

Don't get a fright!
Place the metal cake slice on a dry glass. Rub the polystyrene against your jumper. Place it on the cake slice. Slowly move your finger towards the handle of the cake slice...

What's happening?

When you rub the polystyrene it becomes negatively charged. When you place it on the metal cake slice, the negative particles in the metal will be pushed away as far as possible by the negative particles in the polystyrene, all the way to the handle. Negatively charged particles in one object always react against those in another object. If you touch the cake slice you feel an electric shock. This is because each human being, just like the cake slice, is statically (electrically) charged.

As he neared Damascus on his journey, suddenly a light from heaven flashed around him. He fell to the ground and heard a voice say to him, "Saul, Saul, why do you persecute me?"
Acts 9:3–4

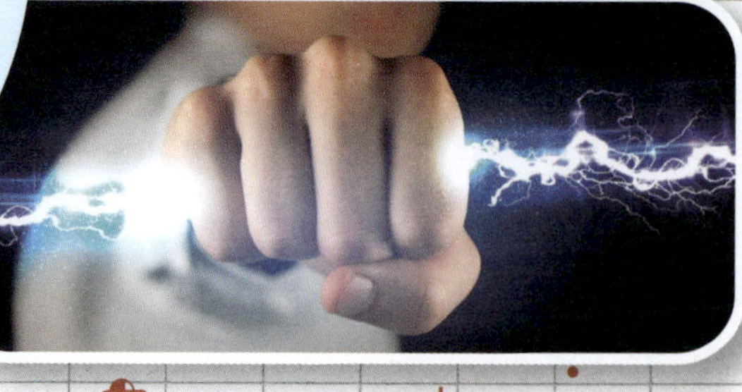

Saul gets a new name: Paul.

FROM ROCK-HARD TO SOFT

You need: raw egg, small bowl, vinegar

Carefully squeeze the egg. What does it feel like? Place the egg in the bowl. Immerse it in vinegar. Leave the egg to stand in the vinegar for 24 hours. Remove the egg from the bowl. Carefully squeeze the egg. What does it feel like now?

But when God, who set me apart from my mother's womb and called me by his grace, was pleased to reveal his Son in me so that I might preach him among the Gentiles.
Galatians 1:15–16a

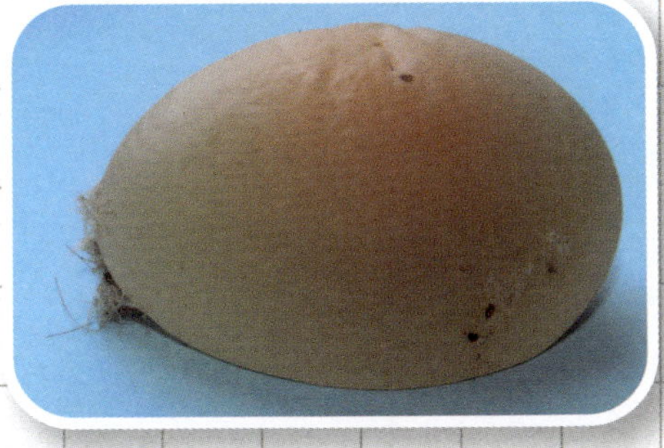

What's happening?

The eggshell is made out of chalk. Chalk is hard. Underneath the shell there is a membrane (thin lining). Vinegar is acidic. Acid dissolves chalk. After 24 hours the eggshell has been dissolved and all that is left is the soft membrane containing the egg white and the yolk.

Soft-shelled eggs are eggs without the hard chalk shell. Young chickens sometimes lay this kind of egg.

WHAT CAN YOU FEEL?

Paul is bitten by a snake ACTS 28

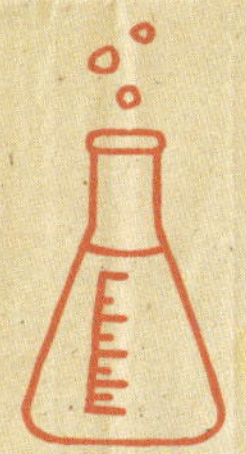

WHAT CAN YOU FEEL?

You need: pair of compasses or divider, cocktail sticks, blindfold (or tea towel), sticky tape, scissors, ruler

Fasten one cocktail stick to each tip of the compasses, partly overlapping. Open up the compasses by moving the tips 4cm (1½in) apart. Blindfold another person. Carefully prick their arm lightly with the two cocktail sticks, 4cm (1½in) apart. How many pricks do they feel? Move the points of your tool so the sticks are only 3cm (1in) apart. Prick again. How many pricks does the blindfolded person feel? Move again so there are 2cm (⅔in) between the points and ask the same question. Repeat (with smaller gaps) until the person only feels one prick. How many mm or cm (or in) are there between the two sticks when they feel just one prick? Try again in a different place, for instance just above the knee, on a finger or on the palm of their hand. Is there any difference?

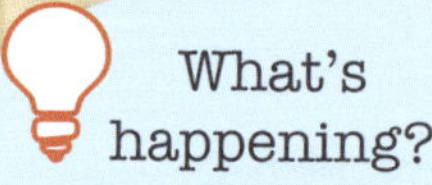

What's happening?

Within our skin there are special cells we use for feeling, called touch receptors. They send a signal to the brain that tells us whether something is hard or soft, warm or cold, rough or smooth. In some areas of our body there are more touch receptors than others. The closer the cocktail sticks are when you feel them as one prick, the more sensitive the skin is in that area.

Paul gathered a pile of brushwood and, as he put it on the fire, a viper, driven out by the heat, fastened itself on his hand.
Acts 28:3

But Paul shook the snake off into the fire and suffered no ill effects.
Acts 28:5

Your bottom is the least sensitive – but don't try this out (ouch!)

TRICK YOUR SENSES

You need: glass of hot water, glass of lukewarm water, glass of cold water

Immerse your index finger in the glass of hot water for ten seconds and dip it straight into the glass of lukewarm water. Does the water feel lukewarm? Immerse your other index finger in the glass of cold water and move it straight into the glass of lukewarm water. What does the lukewarm water feel like now?

What's happening?

Your body adjusts to the temperature and feels the difference. When you moved your finger from the hot to the lukewarm water, your body signalled "colder" to your brain. When you moved your finger from the cold to the lukewarm water your body sent the signal "warmer" to your brain.

When Paul was bitten by the snake he was on the island of Malta. Paul and his travel companions had been shipwrecked near the coast. You can read the story in Acts 27:39–44.

FILLED WITH IMMEASURABLE LOVE

Jesus' love for you EPHESIANS 3

And I pray that you... may have power, together with all the Lord's holy people, to grasp how wide and long and high and deep is the love of Christ...
Ephesians 3:17b, 18

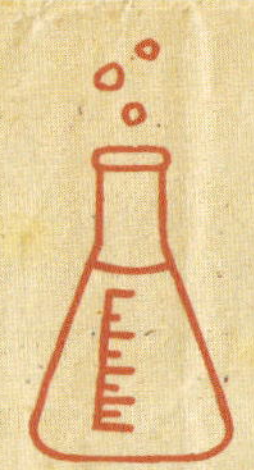

THE GOLDEN RATIO: THE VITRUVIAN MAN

You need: measuring tape, pen and paper

The "Vitruvian Man" drawing by Leonardo da Vinci is world famous. Da Vinci drew this using a theory invented by an architect, Marcus Vitruvius (85–20 BC), who claimed that the height of the body of an adult human is the same as their arm span (the distance between one hand and the other when the arms are completely stretched out). Is your body height the same as your arm span? Measure both and compare!

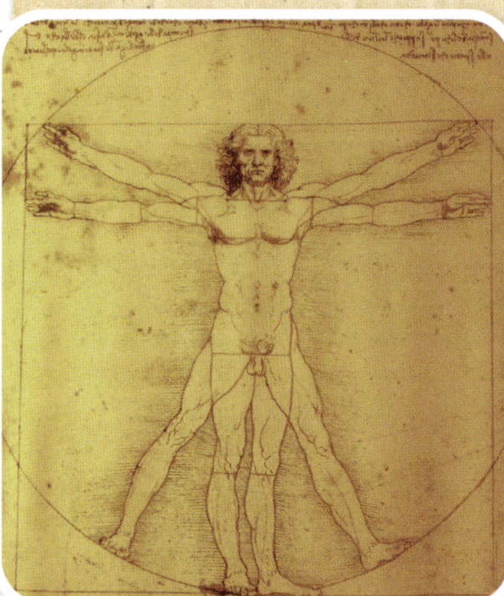

"The Vitruvian Man", drawn by Leonardo da Vinci, fifteenth century

The body of an adult can be divided into eight equal lengths.

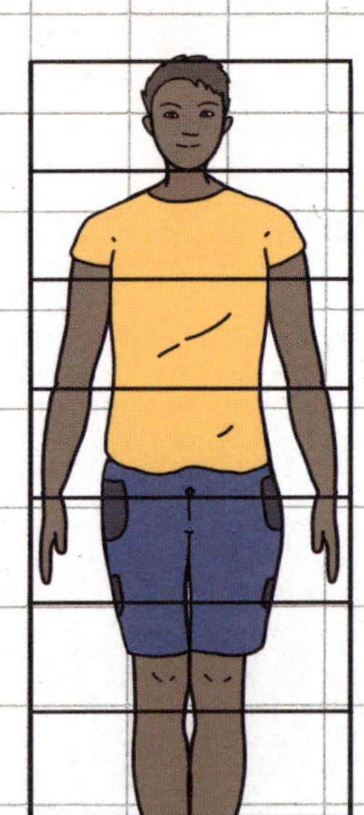

Tip: Measure a parent or other adult and check, or draw a realistic figure of a person using these proportions.

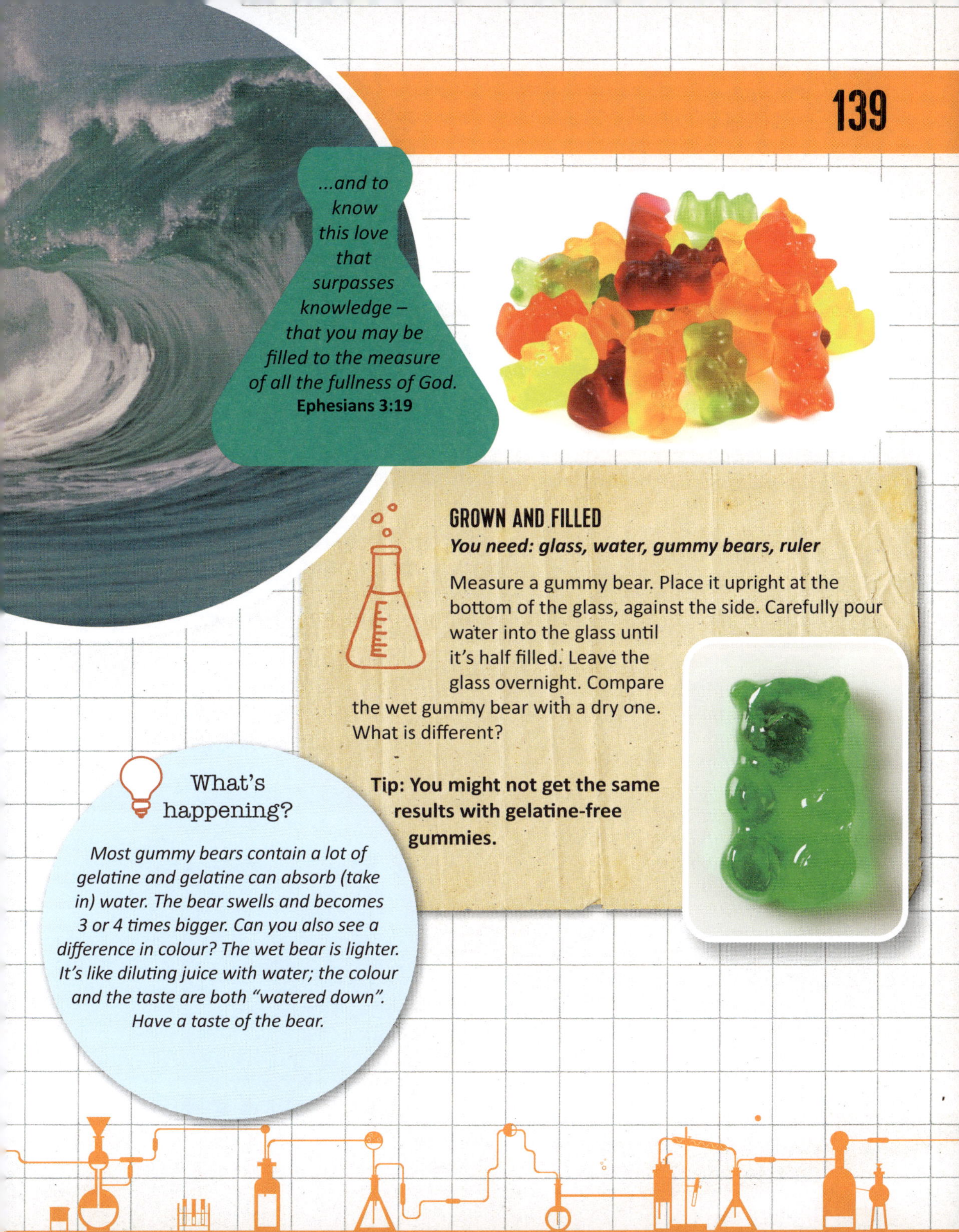

...and to know this love that surpasses knowledge – that you may be filled to the measure of all the fullness of God.
Ephesians 3:19

GROWN AND FILLED

You need: glass, water, gummy bears, ruler

Measure a gummy bear. Place it upright at the bottom of the glass, against the side. Carefully pour water into the glass until it's half filled. Leave the glass overnight. Compare the wet gummy bear with a dry one. What is different?

Tip: You might not get the same results with gelatine-free gummies.

What's happening?

Most gummy bears contain a lot of gelatine and gelatine can absorb (take in) water. The bear swells and becomes 3 or 4 times bigger. Can you also see a difference in colour? The wet bear is lighter. It's like diluting juice with water; the colour and the taste are both "watered down". Have a taste of the bear.

DAZZLING

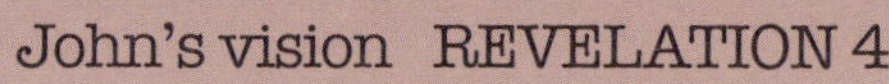

John's vision REVELATION 4

COLOUR AND LIGHT SHOW

You need: plastic lid (of a tub), lots of white PVA glue, various colours of liquid watercolour or food colouring, cocktail sticks, string, hole punch

Spread a layer of glue inside the lid, cover the whole area. Squeeze a drop of each colour onto the glue. Stir with a cocktail stick until you see a lovely pattern of colours.

Watch out: if you stir too long, all the colours will mix and turn brown.

Leave the glue mixture to dry. Be patient, it will take at least a day, depending on the thickness of the layer of glue. You can peel the layer away once the edges have become detached from the lid. Pull the mixture out of the lid. Make a hole with the hole punch and attach the string. Hang your decoration in front of a window in a sunny spot.

At once I was in the Spirit, and there before me was a throne in heaven with someone sitting on it. And the one who sat there had the appearance of jasper and ruby. A rainbow that shone like an emerald encircled the throne. Surrounding the throne were twenty-four other thrones, and seated on them were twenty-four elders. They were dressed in white and had crowns of gold on their heads. From the throne came flashes of lightning, rumblings and peals of thunder. In front of the throne, seven lamps were blazing. These are the seven spirits of God. Also in front of the throne there was what looked like a sea of glass, clear as crystal.

Revelation 4:2–6a

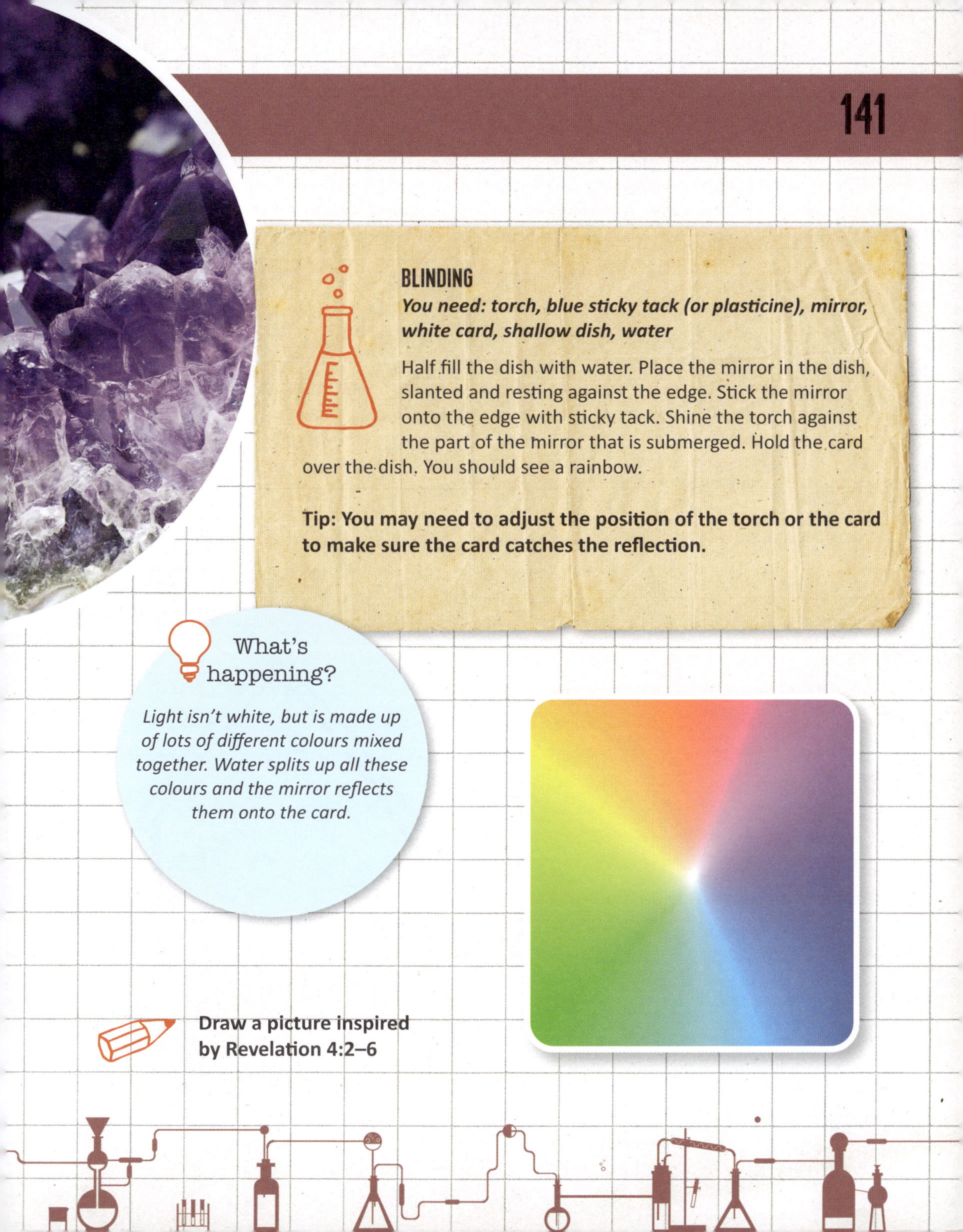

BLINDING

You need: torch, blue sticky tack (or plasticine), mirror, white card, shallow dish, water

Half fill the dish with water. Place the mirror in the dish, slanted and resting against the edge. Stick the mirror onto the edge with sticky tack. Shine the torch against the part of the mirror that is submerged. Hold the card over the dish. You should see a rainbow.

Tip: You may need to adjust the position of the torch or the card to make sure the card catches the reflection.

What's happening?

Light isn't white, but is made up of lots of different colours mixed together. Water splits up all these colours and the mirror reflects them onto the card.

Draw a picture inspired by Revelation 4:2–6

APPENDICES

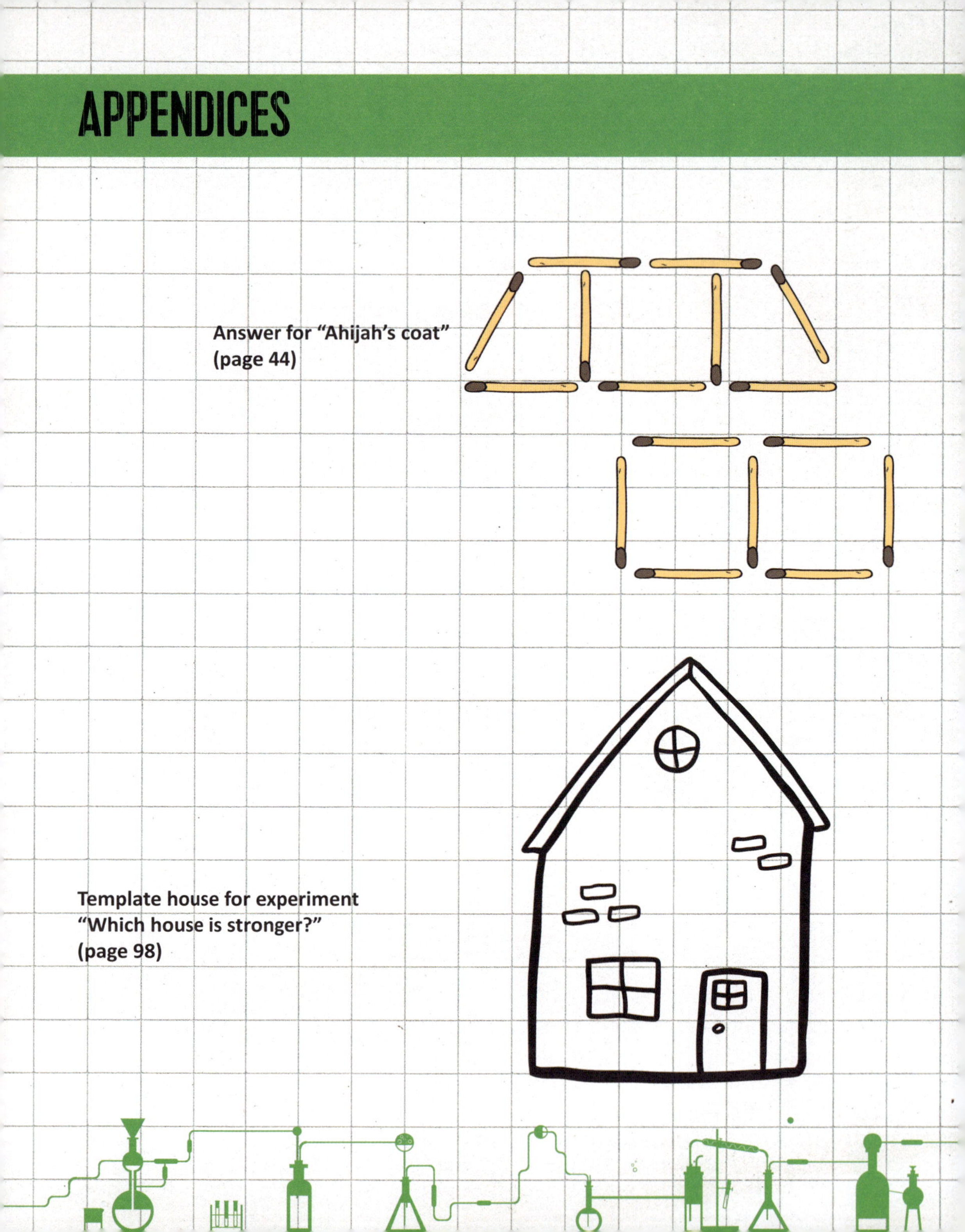

Answer for "Ahijah's coat" (page 44)

Template house for experiment "Which house is stronger?" (page 98)

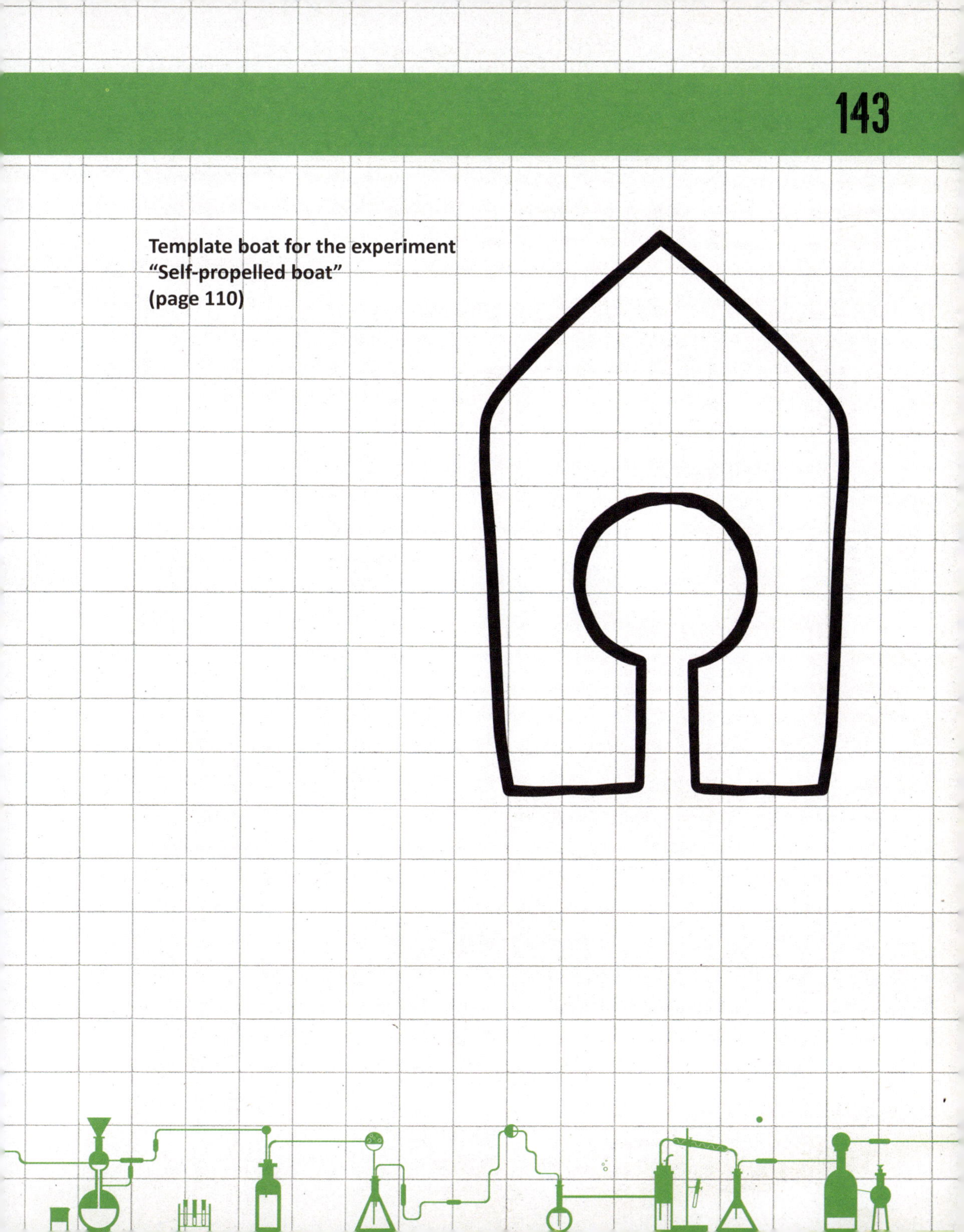

Template boat for the experiment "Self-propelled boat"
(page 110)

OVERVIEW OF BIBLE QUOTATIONS

OVERVIEW OF BIBLE QUOTATIONS

INDEX OF PEOPLE AND THINGS

INDEX OF PEOPLE AND THINGS

NOTES

NOTES

NOTES

NOTES

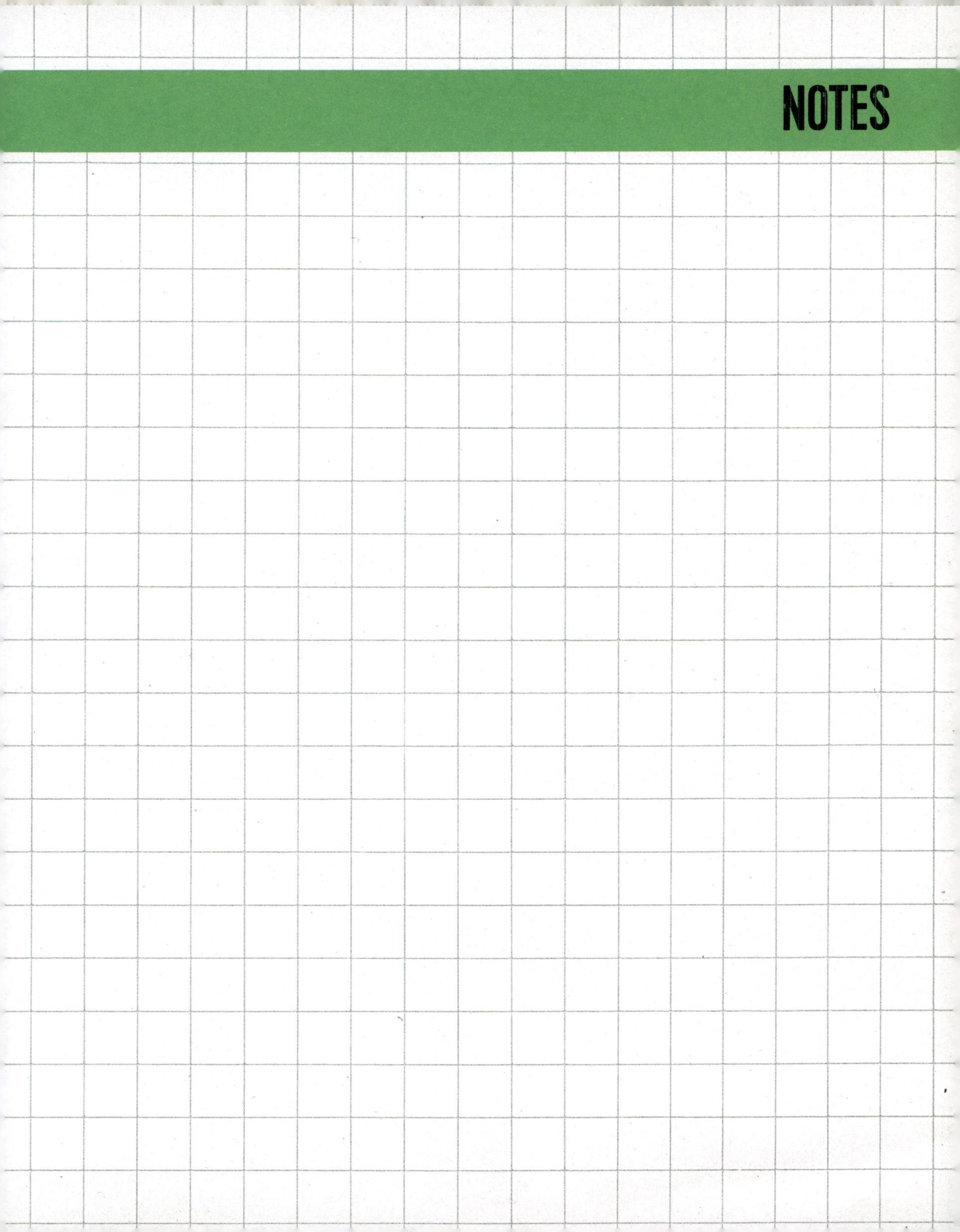
NOTES

NOTES

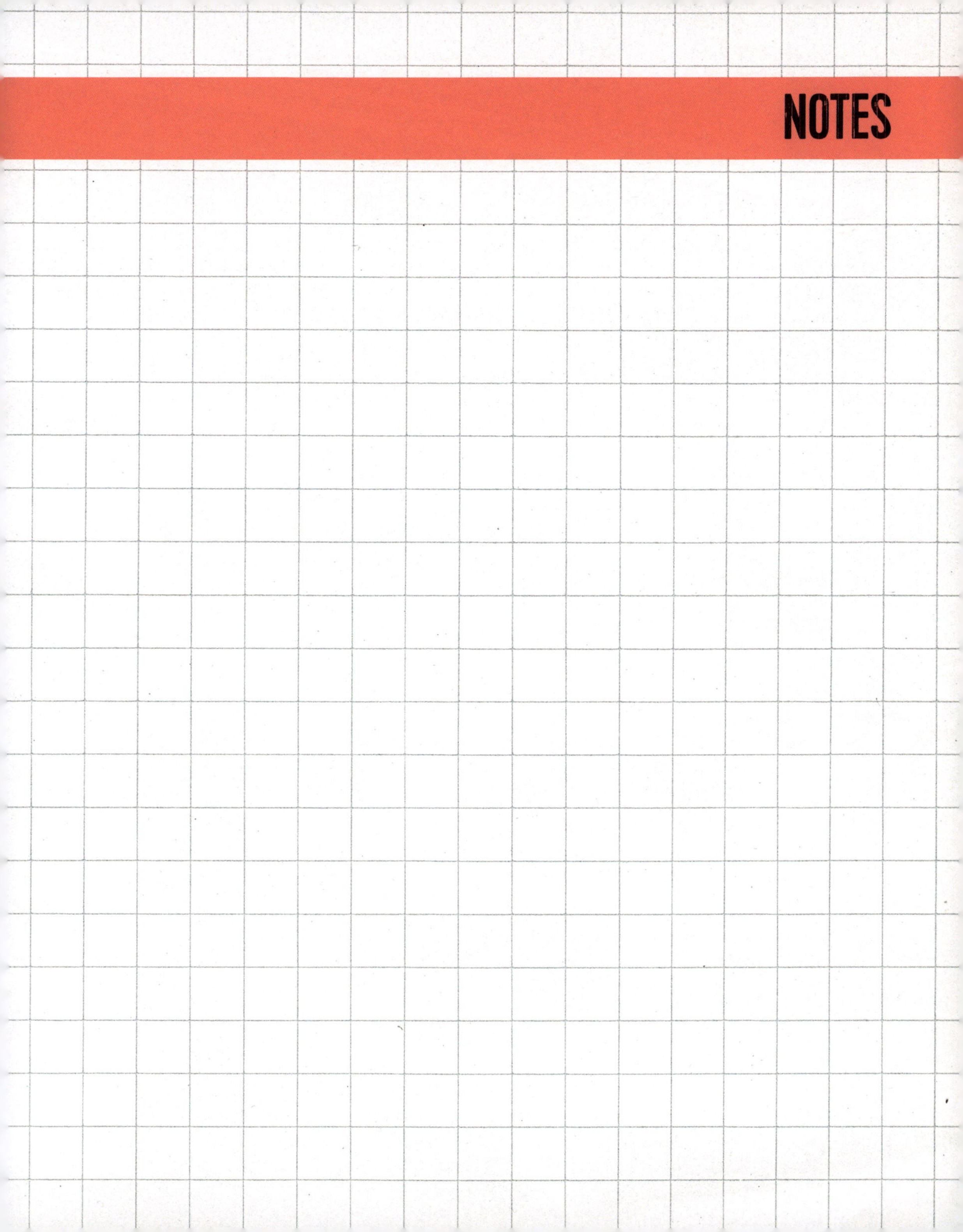
NOTES

IMAGE ACKNOWLEDGMENTS

Bigstock:
pp. 22–23 (goat) © Lilun/bigstockphoto.com
p. 28 (fist) © Milkos/bigstockphoto.com
pp. 30–31 (flames) © studiog/bigstockphoto.com, (burning bush) © Mieszko9/bigstockphoto.com
p. 39 (eggs) © Geshas/bigstockphoto.com, (bridge) © IHB/bigstockphoto.com
p. 40 (marshmallows) © kaiskynet/bigstockphoto.com
p. 44 (matches) © parinya/bigstockphoto.com
p. 45 (salt and pepper) © Ylivdesign/bigstockphoto.com
pp. 48–49 (forest fire) © Lumppini/bigstockphoto.com
p. 53 (bottle) © karandaev/bigstockphoto.com

Dreamstime:
p. 11 (wildflowers) © Frantisek Chmura/Dreamstime.com
pp. 14–15 (DNA) © Kts/Dreamstime.com
pp. 16–17 (wellies) © Darya Petrenko/ Dreamstime.com
p. 17 (oil) © Yekophotostudio/Dreamstime.com, (boat) © Celia Maria Ribeiro Ascenso/Dreamstime.com
p. 19 (storm) © Javarman/Dreamstime.com
p. 21 (iceberg) © Steve Allen/Dreamstime.com
p. 24 (finger on water) © Fireflyphoto/Dreamstime.com
p. 25 (tangerine) © Nevinantes/Dreamstime.com, (tangerine peel) © Vyacheslav Bukhal/Dreamstime.com
pp. 32–33 (sun through clouds) © Skarie20/ Dreamstime.com
p. 34 (apple) © Ducdao/Dreamstime.com
pp. 38–39 (dog and kitten) © Isselee/Dreamstime.com
p. 51 (atom) © Mrjafari/Dreamstime.com
pp. 52–53 (space shuttle launch) © Mikephotos/ Dreamstime.com
pp. 54–55 (girl washing hair) © Nataliia Prokofyeva/ Dreamstime.com
pp. 56–57 (earth and sun) © Jeffplay/Dreamstime.com
pp. 60–61 (jigsaw puzzle) © Micro Vacca/Dreamstime.com, (two girls) © Nicolegardner/Dreamstime.com
p. 61 (marbles) © Dvmsimages/Dreamstime.com
p. 64 (half-peeled orange) © Igor Zakharevich/ Dreamstime.com
pp. 64–65 (scared balloon) © Orlando Florin Rosu/ Dreamstime.com
p. 66 (kneading clay) © Sierpniowka/Dreamstime.com
pp. 66–67 (potter's wheel) © Zojakostina/ Dreamstime.com
p. 70 (whirlpool in glass) © Vitaly Korovin/ Dreamstime.com
pp. 70–71 (sea) © Adazavr/Dreamstime.com
p. 72 (carrots) © Elena Schweitzer/Dreamstime.com
p. 73 (landscape with tree) © Kwiktor/Dreamstime.com
p. 74 (eye) © Tribalium/Dreamstime.com
p. 75 (bat) © Farinoza/Dreamstime.com, (boy feeling throat) © Ulianna19970/Dreamstime.com
p. 79 (girl looking through fingers) © Syda Productions/Dreamstime.com, (optical illusion lines) © Zuberka/Dreamstime.com, (optical illusion spots) Fenix84/Dreamstime.com
p. 80 (boys with string phone) Robert Kneschke/ Dreamstime.com
pp. 80–81 (newspapers) © Oleg Dudko/Dreamstime.com
p. 82 (lighter) © Lightsecond/Dreamstime.com, (burning ice) © Stewart Scott/Dreamstime.com
p. 83 (candles) © Jiradelta/Dreamstime.com
pp. 84–85 (sugar crystals) © Penchan Pumilla/ Dreamstime.com
p. 86 (quadrant) © Garth Grimmer/Dreamstime.com
pp. 86–87 (telescope against sky) © Allexander/ Dreamstime.com
pp. 88–89 (splashing water) © Okea/Dreamstime.com
p. 89 (dove) © Vitaly Titov/Dreamstime.com
p. 90 (marbles in sand) © Pxlxl/Dreamstime.com
pp. 90–91 (girl with phone) © Traimak Ivan/ Dreamstime.com
p. 91 (falling meteorite) © Ffang/Dreamstime.com, (meteorite debris) © Nuttapong/Dreamstime.com
p. 92 (egg experiment 1) © Borzywoj/Dreamstime.com
pp. 92–93 (optical illusion cube) © Ffatserifade/ Dreamstime.com
p. 93 (egg experiment 2, egg experiment 3, egg experiment 4) © Borzywoj/Dreamstime.com
pp. 94–95 (girl with pinwheel) © Photographerlondon/Dreamstime.com
pp. 98–99 (foundation) © Wittybear/Dreamstime.com
p. 99 (wooden building blocks) © Boris15/ Dreamstime.com
p. 100 (plant in container) © Olesya Tseytlin/ Dreamstime.com
pp. 100–101 (seedlings) © Joystockphoto.com/ Dreamstime.com
p. 101 (mustard seed) © Petarneychev/Dreamstime.com
pp. 102–103 (girls upside down) © Yarruta/

Dreamstime.com
pp. 104–105 (girl with wheelchair) © Bubutu/Dreamstime.com
p. 106 (red cabbage) © Nevinantes/Dreamstime.com
pp. 106–107 (wine) © Yurok/Dreamstime.com
p. 107 (tea glass) © Weber11/Dreamstime.com, (tea leaves) © Leung Cho Pan/Dreamstime.com
p. 108 (leprosy hand) © Tawatchai Khid-arn/Dreamstime.com, (rattle) © Burnel1/Dreamstime.com
pp. 108–109 (bacteria) © Alexander Raths/Dreamstime.com
pp. 110–11 (water and sky) © Chriskiely/Dreamstime.com
p. 111 (view from plane) © Thetaweeyo/Dreamstime.com
pp. 112–13 (girl doing eye test) © Karelnoppe/Dreamstime.com
p. 113 (toy bricks) © Veleknez/Dreamstime.com
pp. 114–15 (boy wading) © Esben Hansen/Dreamstime.com
p. 115 (pond skater) © Karelgallas/Dreamstime.com
p. 117 (colour theory) © Yana Bolbot/Dreamstime.com
p. 118 (burning match) © Chaoss/Dreamstime.com
pp. 118–19 (washing machine) © Yuriy Chaban/Dreamstime.com
p. 122 (bean germination) © Filipe Varela/Dreamstime.com
p. 125 (3D image) © Vicnt/Dreamstime.com
p. 127 (play-dough tubs) © Chernetskaya/Dreamstime.com
pp. 128–29 (dancing children) © Katarzyna Bialasiewicz/Dreamstime.com
p. 129 (salt) © Valeriidekhtiarenko/Dreamstime.com, (cola) © Joanna Zopoth Lipiejko/Dreamstime.com
p. 130 (boy eating cereal) © Wavebreakmedia Ltd/Dreamstime.com
pp. 130–31 (body and veins) © Skypixel/Dreamstime.com
p. 131 (blood cells) © Frenta/Dreamstime.com
p. 132 (scourer) © Todsaporn Bunmuen/Dreamstime.com
p. 133 (steel wool) © Timages/Dreamstime.com
p. 134 (fist with lightning) © Ratz Attila/Dreamstime.com
pp. 134–35 (lightning) © Anettphoto/Dreamstime.com
pp. 136–37 (snake) © Heirbornstud/Dreamstime.com
p. 138 (Vitruvian Man) © Piotr Paczyński/Dreamstime.com
pp. 138–39 (wave) © Jinyoung Lee/Dreamstime.com
p. 139 (gummy bears) © Kheng Ho Toh/Dreamstime.com, (green gummy bear) © Ajafoto/Dreamstime.com
p. 141 (colour spectrum) © Lookzone/Dreamstime.com

iStock:
pp. 12–13 (girl with balloon) © Tom Merton/istockphoto.com
pp. 18–19 (landscape with rainbow) © Sven_Stroop/istockphoto.com
pp. 20–21 (girl blowing bubbles) © Rawpixel/istockphoto.com
pp. 24–25 (boy in life jacket) © EVAfotografie/istockphoto.com
p. 22 (fingerprint) © puflic_senior/istockphoto.com
pp. 26–27 (jealous emoji) © yayayoyo/istockphoto.com
pp. 28–29 (fighting boys) © vesmil/istockphoto.com
pp. 34–35 (sad girl) © ridvan_celik/istockphoto.com
pp. 36–37 (man with shofar) © John Theodor/istockphoto.com
pp. 40–41 (boy showing muscles) © PeopleImages/istockphoto.com
pp. 42–43 (students doing experiment) © Django/istockphoto.com
pp. 44–45 (girl in jumper) © D-Keine/istockphoto.com
pp. 46–47 (boy with crown) © Imgorthand/istockphoto.com
pp. 50–51 (praying girl) © undefined undefined/istockphoto.com
p. 53 (coin) © LeksusTuss/istockphoto.com
p. 54 (penny) © coopder1/istockphoto.com
p. 54 (Euro cent) © malerapaso/istockphoto.com
p. 54 (US cent) © wrangel/istockphoto.com
pp. 58–59 (boy with bandage) © Thongchai Saisanguanwong/istockphoto.com
pp. 62–63 (sealed food) © sorapol1150/istockphoto.com
pp. 68–69 (tomatoes) © SimonSkafar/istockphoto.com
p. 71 (children with blender) © vm/istockphoto.com
pp. 72–73 (stubborn boy) © LightFieldStudios/istockphoto.com
pp. 74–75 (boy covering mouth) © Sadeugra/istockphoto.com
pp. 76–77 (pregnant woman) © belchonock/istockphoto.com

IMAGE ACKNOWLEDGMENTS

pp. 78–79 (thoughtful boy) © Juanmonino/
istockphoto.com
pp. 82–83 (lighthouse) © FinnBrandt/istockphoto.com
p. 94 (boy with pinwheels) © AshleyWiley/
istockphoto.com
pp. 96–97 (boys sharing secret) © PeopleImages/
istockphoto.com
pp. 116–17 (dark clouds) © baona/istockphoto.com
p. 119 (glass of water) © ManuWe/istockphoto.com
pp. 120–21 (sisters snuggling) © AmeliaFox/
istockphoto.com
pp. 122–23 (girl with magnifying glass) © Ghislain &
Marie David de Lossy/istockphoto.com
p. 123 (roots cracking tarmac) © itman__47/
istockphoto.com
p. 124 (3D glasses) © subjug/istockphoto.com,
pp. 124–25 (boy with binoculars) © Jasonfang/
istockphoto.com
pp. 126–27 (hot air balloon) © anyaberkut/
istockphoto.com
p. 127 (girl on trampoline) © ferrantraite/istockphoto.com
pp. 132–33 (boy with Bible) © aldomurillo/
istockphoto.com
pp. 140–41 (amethyst) © LVV/istockphoto.com

Shutterstock:
p. 118 (girl blowing out candle) © dragon_fang/
shutterstock.com
p. 124 (children with 3D glasses) © Luis Louro/
shutterstock.com

All other images and illustrations are copyright © 2018 Uitgeverij Columbus, apart from the following, which are in the public domain:
pp. 10–11 ("The Blue Marble": Earth seen from Apollo 17) Taken by NASA/Apollo 17
p. 135 (soft egg) Timo Rieg/Wikipedia Creative Commons